FASTING

&

FEASTING

Erin Davis

FASTING

FEASTING

40 Devotions to Satisfy the Hungry Heart

B&H
PUBLISHING
NASHVILLE, TENNESSEE

Published by B&H Publishing Group
Nashville, Tennessee

Dewey Decimal Classification: 242.64
Subject Heading: DEVOTIONAL
LITERATURE / FOOD / FASTING

Cover design by Studio Nth, LLC. Illustration by
HappyPictures and Cobisimo, shutterstock. Author
photo by Katie Bollinger with *Revive Our Hearts*.

1 2 3 4 5 6 7 • 26 25 24 23 22

To my Aunt Rhonda, whose love for food inspired mine and whose love for Jesus makes me hungry for more of Him.

Aunt Rhonda's Perfect Pie Crust

In a glass bowl add 2 cups of all-purpose flour plus 1/2 tsp. salt.

Make a well in the center with a spoon.

Pour 1/2 cup plus 1 tbl. Crisco oil into the well and begin mixing with a fork.

After partially mixed, add 1/4 cup milk and mix with your fingers until it forms a ball.

Divide in half and form 2 balls.

Roll each ball between two sheets of wax paper.

Flip over into a pie pan.

Peel off second sheet of wax paper.

Fill with filling (preferably fresh peaches).

Take the second ball and peel off one sheet of wax paper.

Flip over onto filling to form second crust.

Crimp edge and bake.

Enjoy!

ACKNOWLEDGMENTS

Though I am honored to have my name on the cover of this book, I acknowledge the many others who made it happen, made it better, and made it beautiful. I offer my deepest and most heartfelt appreciation to the many gifted and gracious people whose invisible fingerprints are all over the pages of this work including:

Jason Davis, as my husband and better two-thirds, you are my first and favorite editor. You patiently listened to this project at every phase. You are my most faithful champion. I adore you.

Eli, Noble, Judah, and Ezra Davis, you are the apple of my eye. You are patient with me as I spend countless hours behind the screen and serve too many plates of pizza bites to meet my deadlines. I love you more than buttered popcorn.

Ashley Gorman, your precision with words and fidelity to Scripture impress me. You may be the silent partner in this project, but I heard your voice loud and clear. Thank you for ensuring that every word counts.

Dear Reader, I've thought of you every day of this project. I've imagined your trials and triumphs related to food and faith and longed for you to find lasting satisfaction. Thank you for picking up this book.

Thank you for reading it. And thank you for realizing all I have to offer you is Jesus. *He is enough.*

Jesus, truly You satisfy the longing soul, and the hungry soul You fill with good things (Ps. 107:9). I love You and cannot wait to feast at Your banqueting table.

CONTENTS

INTRODUCTION

There are times when a warm croissant, a bright bowl of fruit, or a steaming cup of coffee feel like perfect, God-given gifts. There are other moments, perhaps more frequent, when food feels like our enemy and our relationship with it becomes a vortex of regret, frustration, and shame.

We read food labels, count calories, and keep lists of favorite recipes, but have you ever stopped to ponder: What does God's Word say about food? The answer might surprise you. It will certainly delight you.

When it comes to what the Bible says about my relationship with food, two words from Mark 9 whet my own appetite to understand. (You'll hear more about this on Day 1.) Like the first bite of chocolate cake, they left me craving more and sent me searching for:

- Other passages that call God's people to fast
- Other examples where the Bible uses food to teach us spiritual principles
- Other times when God invites His people to feast.

I found that God's Word is a smorgasbord that truly satisfies. I am so grateful we will spend the next forty days digging in together.

This book isn't a call to fast for the next forty days, nor is it a call to strictly feast. For now I hope you'll simply soak in God's Word and seek to understand His heart for how food and faith intersect. Sip slowly on Bible passages like a perfect cup of coffee. Really chew on the lessons God is teaching you through His Word.

Each daily devotional finishes with "Setting the Table" and "Inviting the Feast." The inspiration for those sections came from an unforgettable prayer I heard a long time ago. If I close my eyes and try to picture her, I cannot see the face of the woman I first heard offer these words to Jesus, but the memory of her prayer has stayed with me. I've repeated her prayer many times since. I hope you'll do the same.

Lord, we've set the table. We ask you to bring the feast.

Isn't that the Christian life in one bite? We do what we can. We bring our best intentions, our brightest devotions, our purest worship to Jesus as acts of setting the table. Then we wait with anticipation for Him to bring the feast, to fill our hearts with His truth, to fill our homes with life rhythms that truly honor Him. He always does. He always will.

You can set the table right now by opening your Bible and telling God you want to hear from Him. Abandon your ideas about what your relationship with food is "supposed to be." Lay down your guilt about what it has not been in the past. And then commit to meet with Him daily for the next forty days, expecting to be filled.

The Bible celebrates food as a gift while simultaneously inviting us to surrender every area of our lives to Christ's authority—including what we put on our plates. Rather than the yo-yo of loving food and then hating it, Scripture invites us into a different rhythm—**the rhythm of fasting and feasting.**

Hungry to Know Him More,
Erin

THIS KIND

And when He had come into the house, His disciples asked Him privately, "Why could we not cast it out?" So He said to them, "This kind can come out by nothing but prayer and fasting."

—Mark 9:28–29 NKJV

My life has been changed by a footnote. ~~Mark 9 focuses on an uncomfortable story about a daddy and his demon-possessed boy.~~ Scratch that. The real focus of this passage, of every passage, is Jesus. This account puts His unmatched power over the things that torment us on full display.

READ MARK 9:14–29.

As remarkable as these events are, if you're familiar with the Gospels, you know they're not exactly outliers. The Bible records so many examples of Jesus healing the sick, driving out the demonic, and even (more than once) raising the dead. Maybe that's why this particular miracle didn't arrest my heart until my eyes drifted to the footnotes.

Scan the footnotes of Mark 9 for yourself. In reference to verse 29, do you find a notation that adds "and fasting"?

Some older translations of Scripture leave these two vital words in the text, while the rest relegate Christ's mention of fasting to an afterthought at the bottom of the page. For the sake of time, I won't pull on the thread that unravels the why. But I will focus on what matters most—*we all have a "this kind."*

The boy in this passage was controlled by a dark spirit that responded to prayer and fasting and nothing else. Not fretting. Not begging. Not bargaining. No, Jesus was clear, "This kind can come out by nothing but prayer and fasting."

Today, as we sit with our Bibles open, I wonder what "this kinds" you face. Is it a broken relationship that cannot be made right by your best efforts and deepest longings? A bruise on your heart that stays tender no matter how much time goes by? A pattern of sin you cannot break? A root of bitterness you cannot wrench free from the soil? A need you cannot meet? An enemy you cannot defeat?

Let's pause together for a moment and ask the Lord. *What are we most desperate to see driven out of our lives?*

With your "this kind" in mind, take a second look at Mark 9.

> When they came to the disciples, they saw a large crowd around them and scribes disputing with them. When the whole crowd saw him, they were amazed and ran to greet him. He asked them, "What are you arguing with them about?"
>
> Someone from the crowd answered him, "Teacher, I brought my son to you. He has a spirit that makes him unable to speak. Whenever it seizes him, it throws him down, and he foams at the mouth, grinds his teeth, and becomes rigid. I asked your disciples to drive it out, but they couldn't." (vv. 14–18)

Our attention is naturally drawn to the description of the boy convulsing. But look past the drama of his condition and the crowd that clamored for a miracle. Find the disciples. Can't you picture them standing sheepishly in the middle of the melee? Can't you see their eyes drop to their sandals as Jesus declared, "You unbelieving generation, how long will I be with you? How long must I put up with you?"

Can't you almost hear Him sigh as He said, "Bring him to me" (v. 19)?

Why was Jesus so uncharacteristically exasperated? Surely He was not mad at the boy who had been possessed since childhood (v. 21) or the dad who tenderly whimpered, "I do believe; help my unbelief!" (v. 24). Could it be that His disciples had tried to solve this problem in their own strength? That they'd looked for a quick solution that allowed them to bypass admitting their desperate need for His help?

Sin has put every one of us on an uphill battle with pride. Prayer is not our default. We are ever grasping for bootstraps to pull ourselves up by, solutions dependent on our elbow grease, or effortless ways out of trouble.

Yet the "this kinds" remain.

Fasting is not just one more way we can wiggle our way out of the trials that constrict us. **God is far too good and too sovereign to be controlled.** Fasting is a step of surrender, a way to showcase that the "this kinds" in our life are beyond us. It's an outward expression of our inner desire to see God do what we cannot. Fasting throws our hands and our eyes up to the Lord as if to say, "I am powerless here, but You are able. You are God. I cannot move another step in this thing without You."

Do you identify with the tired father today? Are you worn out from trying to solve your biggest problems in your own strength? Consider this: Have prayer and fasting been your first and most often deployed weapon, or are they relegated to the footnotes of your life?

Maybe you see yourself in the disciples. You've rubbed plenty of elbow grease into an area of woundedness or weakness only to find it still festering. Do you shake your head and wonder, "Why couldn't [I] drive it out?" (v. 28). My question remains the same: Have prayer and fasting been your first and most often deployed weapon, or are they relegated to the footnotes of your life?

We all have "this kinds." This side of heaven we always will. But Jesus will always be able to drive out what we cannot. We fast and pray to let go of our strength and to tap into His.

SETTING THE TABLE, INVITING THE FEAST

*Use the prayer prompts below to ask the Lord
to do an abundant work in your life.*

Setting the Table

*Jesus, as I consider Your Word, the "this kinds" that come to my
mind are . . .*

_____

_____

_____

_____

_____

_____

_____

_____

_____

_____

_____

_____

_____

_____

_____

_____

_____

_____

Inviting the Feast

Lord, I need You. I cannot fix these things on my own. I acknowledge You as God—as the only One powerful enough to loosen the grip of the strongholds that have overtaken me.

Rewrite your list from above using this prompt: Lord, I release my attempts to control _____ and ask for Your help.

_____

_____

_____

_____

_____

_____

_____

_____

_____

_____

_____

_____

_____

_____

_____

_____

_____

_____

_____

FEASTING

TASTE AND SEE

Taste and see that the LORD is good. How happy is the person who
takes refuge in him! You who are his holy ones, fear the LORD,
for those who fear him lack nothing. Young lions lack food and go
hungry, but those who seek the LORD will not lack any good thing.

—Psalm 34:8–10

I magine a world where Christmas comes three times a day—a steady stream of gifts all day, every day. Exciting, right? Now take the mental leap with me from that scenario to your kitchen table. Picture the pile of presents God has delivered to that well-worn spot.

Recall Thanksgiving dinners loaded with juicy turkeys and steaming sides. Remember special birthday dinners where your family has blown out the candles atop so many cakes. Think of Sunday suppers and pizza nights, spilled milk, and sticky oatmeal gloop.

In hindsight those meals come to mind with a warm glow around them, don't they? Have you ever wondered why food is involved in so many of our best memories and most cherished relationships? Have you ever considered if that's by design instead of by default?

God never just fills our bellies. *He fills our homes. He fills our hearts.*

READ PSALM 34.

My own dining room table is a hand-me-down from my granny. She bought it in the sixties at a yard sale and stripped it and refinished it herself. It needs to be sanded and finished once again, but I can't bear to erase the spot where the stain from her coffee cup remains. It's a reminder of the blessings God gave me through her.

Many childhood memories involve the table. Some are fancy—candlelit meals eaten on fine china on Christmas Eve. Others are more pedestrian—piles of spaghetti on paper plates, ham sammies with the crust cut off. *All of them are gifts, given to me by a God who loves me.*

When David wanted to express his gratitude for God's blessings, he used food as a frame of reference. He could have said, "Look and see that the LORD is good." We can surely see God's gifts all around us. He could have said, "Listen and see that the LORD is good." We hear His goodness in a child's laughter, in a nightingale's song, in the roar of a waterfall or the dribble of a mountain stream. But David chose an alternate sense to call us to worship. He chose our sense of taste.

Taste and see that the LORD is good. (v. 8)

A few chapters later in Psalm 103, David uses eating imagery again to remind us of God's blessings.

He satisfies you with good things;
your youth is renewed like the eagle. (v. 5)

Satisfaction. Renewed energy. These are the benefits of food. What if each bite is a missionary, sent to remind us who He is and what He has done?

Here's a truth so simple we miss it daily—food is a blessing from God. Let me say it louder for the people in the back—food is a blessing from God!

We live in a culture with a volatile relationship with food. Either food is everything, the key that unlocks a happy, fulfilling life or food is the enemy, a monster we must tame at any cost. Perhaps it's because our bellies experience true hunger so rarely (if ever) that we forget that fundamentally food is a gift, graciously provided by a generous God so that we might taste and see that He is good.

Your morning cup of coffee? That's a gift.

Your breakfast? Yep, that's a gift, too.

Did you have a yummy salad for lunch or a sandwich with a bag of chips? Did you bless the Lord for giving you the gift of food once again?

As you make dinner plans, are you fixated on the ingredients you don't have or the fact that you have hungry mouths to feed again? Or are you reminded that God is good? That He still has good things in store for you today?

Don't veer into guilt. That's not the action step the psalmist calls us to. Instead, ask the Lord to help you see food as a gift from Him, to use what you taste to help you see—He really is good. "He satisfies you with good things."

SETTING THE TABLE, INVITING THE FEAST

*Use the prayer prompts below to ask the Lord
to do an abundant work in your life.*

Setting the Table

*Jesus, as I consider Your Word, I am reminded that You are a good
God. Thank You for the many blessings You've given me today
including . . .*

_____

_____

_____

_____

_____

Inviting the Feast

*Lord, I forget that even the food on my table is a gift from You.
Teach me to be mindful of Your many blessings. Help me more
often to taste and see that You are good.*

_____

_____

_____

_____

_____

_____

_____

....

....

BECOMING A SPIRITUAL TRIATHLETE

Then Jesus was led up by the Spirit into the wilderness to be tempted by the devil. After he had fasted forty days and forty nights, he was hungry.

—Matthew 4:1–2

Having a strong personal aversion to discomfort, I greatly admire those with the fortitude to push their bodies to the limit. Soldiers who fight through the rigor of basic training have my mad respect. Triathletes with the inner grit required to swim, cycle, and run mile after mile earn my genuine awe.

Though you won't catch me "pushing through the pain" or winning feats of strength, I hope to become a spiritual triathlete, capable of running the race of faith with great endurance.

READ MATTHEW 4:1–11.

Three observations jump off the page at me about the timing of Jesus' wilderness fast.

First, the fast followed a moment of remarkable victory. Matthew 3 records Jesus' baptism (vv. 13–17). The heavens opened, the Spirit descended, and the Father boomed His approval from heaven. This was a supernatural event! Still, Jesus did not immediately begin His earthly ministry after His submersion in the Jordan. There is a gap between His commissioning and His mission. *Jesus spent that gap fasting.*

Second, the fast preceded an intense battle with the devil. This was a series of skirmishes in a war of cosmic significance. We don't see the Enemy come at Jesus this directly or doggedly again in the Gospel accounts. Because He is sovereign, Jesus knew the fight was coming. Fasting is how He chose to prepare.

Third, Jesus fasted for forty days and forty nights. Let's park there together today.

Have you ever noticed that the number forty is a pattern repeated often in Scripture?

Moses lived forty years in Egypt (Acts 7:23) and forty years in the desert before he was chosen to lead Israel out of slavery (Acts 7:30). Twice he met with the Lord on Mount Sinai for a period of forty days and forty nights (Exod. 24:18; 34:28). The second time he entered a dramatic fast, "he did not eat food or drink water" while he "wrote the Ten Commandments, the words of the covenant, on the tablets" (Exod. 34:28).

The Israelite spies investigated the promised land for forty days (Num. 13:25), and when the children of Israel responded with disbelief, they were sentenced to a period of wandering for—you guessed it—forty years. Jonah prophesied that Nineveh would be overthrown in forty days (Jonah 3:4). Ezekiel laid on his right side for forty days in lament for the sins of Judah (Ezek. 4:6). Elijah fasted for forty days as he journeyed to Mount Horeb (1 Kings 19:8).

In each case, the number forty represents a period of great testing. More often than not, day forty-one brought spiritual battles and kingdom victories.

Flip back to Matthew 4. Zero in on verse 17.

> From then on Jesus began to preach, "Repent, because the kingdom of heaven has come near."

Soldiers train to fight. Triathletes train to compete. Jesus fasted to prepare to turn the world upside down.

Fitness experts have long celebrated the value of a forty-day regimen to realign our habits. If this is how realignment works in a person's body, it's not hard to believe that the same might be true for a person's spirit. The Bible doesn't specify that every fast must last for forty days. Perhaps the significance of forty is less about the number and more about the commitment it represents. A forty-day fast is more than a fleeting notion; it goes beyond the inconvenience of a hunger pang or two. A forty-day fast requires an all-in commitment of body and spirit.

At the moment I'm writing this sentence, I've completed two forty-day juice fasts. Both preceded the launch of ministry efforts so significant and demanding, rigorous "training" was required. The length of the fast tested my commitment. The intensity of the fast led me to a place of total dependency on Jesus I wouldn't have acknowledged on day ten or twenty.

Though always uncomfortable, fasting is a discipline God can use to help us develop our spiritual muscles and prepare us for the battles that lie ahead. Do you want to withstand the Enemy's attacks with faith and fortitude? Consider Jesus. Give Him your awe, but don't stop there. As a follower of Jesus who wants to live like Jesus lived, take time today to consider: Is there a pattern in His forty-day fast worth repeating in your own life?

SETTING THE TABLE, INVITING THE FEAST

*Use the prayer prompts below to ask the Lord
to do an abundant work in your life.*

Setting the Table

Jesus, I am amazed at Your ability to forgo comfort and withstand temptation. Help me see where my spiritual muscles are weak and embrace the discomfort required to grow in You.

Write down any weaknesses the Lord brings to mind.

_____

_____

_____

_____

_____

_____

_____

_____

_____

_____

_____

_____

_____

_____

_____

Inviting the Feast

Lord, I don't want the Christian life to be uncomfortable. I often resist the Holy Spirit when He moves to stretch me in the areas I need to be developed. Show me some ways I can grow in this.

_____

_____

_____

_____

_____

_____

_____

_____

_____

_____

Write down any spiritual disciplines the Lord brings to mind.

_____

_____

_____

_____

_____

_____

_____

_____

_____

FEASTNG

A DIFFERENT KIND OF LEFTOVERS

Then Jesus took the loaves, and after giving thanks he distributed them to those who were seated—so also with the fish, as much as they wanted.

—John 6:11

If you've ever raised a man cub, you can empathize with my battle with the grocery budget. The cost to feed four sons (plus my husband and me) is staggering. On an average week we go through two gallons of milk, six boxes of cereal, two loaves of bread, and four dozen eggs. (That's just breakfast, ya'll!) My boys can flat out *eat*. We are blessed to have enough resources to feed them as often as they wish. My children have never experienced true hunger.

Still they wake up every morning worried they will have to.

"Mom, what's for breakfast?"

"Mom, can I have a snack?"

"Mom, what's for lunch?"

"Mom, do we have any snacks?"

"Mom, what's for dinner?"

"Can I have a snack? Can I have a snack? Can I have a snack?"

Every road trip I hear the same worried question, often before our car has even left the driveway. "Buuuut what will weeee eaaaat?"

It's funny and frustrating but also revealing. Don't *we* have a constant, gnawing fear that this will be the day the Lord forgets about our needs or makes us go without?

READ JOHN 6:1–15.

The crowds had seen that Jesus could do miracles (John 6:2), but watching the work of the Divine on behalf of someone else only increases our heart pangs. Surely each person wanted a miracle of his own. In this way these people are an archetype for us. We each have a longing, deep and urgent, to have Jesus fill us up.

Before the approaching crowd reached Him and gathered to hear His hillside sermon, Jesus turned to His trusted disciple Philip and asked, "Where will we buy bread so that these people can eat?" (v. 5). As verse 6 tells us, Jesus didn't pose the question because He did not know where to find food for the crowds but rather to see if *Philip* knew where the provision would come from. The needs of the crowd didn't surprise Jesus. Like a mom preparing snacks for a road trip, He knew they needed to be fed (v. 6).

> Philip answered him, "Two hundred denarii worth of bread wouldn't be enough for each of them to have a little." (v. 7)

Philip had the facts right, but where was his faith? He was at the wedding at Cana where Jesus turned water into wine (John 2:11). He had seen Jesus heal the official's son at Capernaum (John 4:46–54).

He'd watched the lame man leap up from his sickbed at the Pool of Bethesda (John 5:1–8). Yet he didn't believe Jesus could meet the scope of needs that were walking toward them. It just took a few hungry followers to expose the truth: Philip operated out of scarcity.

Scarcity, it seems, is part and parcel of being broken people in a broken world. My boys' fear that they won't have enough to eat isn't based on experience. Sin has stamped a scarcity mindset onto their little hearts. And it's stamped onto yours.

While the primary lesson of this story in John 6 is about Jesus Himself being our provision (more on that later), let's pause here and consider a secondary lesson. Let's examine how our own attitudes toward food point toward wider issues of faith. What does chronic overeating say about our walk with the Lord? Or using food as a constant source of indulgence? Or fear of calories? Or obsession with eating organic? Or deep shame attached to that slice of cheesecake you ate last night? Often these are not just food issues. *These are faith issues*—reminders that only Jesus can fully satisfy.

Back to the hillside.

> Then Jesus took the loaves, and after giving thanks he distributed them to those who were seated—so also with the fish, *as much as they wanted.*
>
> When they were full, he told his disciples, "*Collect the leftovers* so that nothing is wasted." (vv. 11–12, emphasis added)

This isn't a fictional story. Those baskets of leftovers were as real as the book you are holding in your hands. But aren't they also a bit metaphorical? Like my sweet sons, we wake up every day with longings. The work we've seen Christ do in the past often isn't enough to carry the day. We fret we will be forced to go without.

Those are the facts. Here's where we can put our faith:

- "He satisfies you with good things" (Ps. 103:5).
- "He does not withhold the good" (Ps. 84:11).
- He meets all of our "needs according to his riches in glory in Christ Jesus" (Phil. 4:19).

This miracle reveals more than Jesus' ability to fill us up. It showcases that He can fill us to the point of overflow, and if we let it, it can shift our hearts from scarcity to abundance.

SETTING THE TABLE, INVITING THE FEAST

Use the prayer prompts below to ask the Lord
to do an abundant work in your life.

Setting the Table

Jesus, are there food patterns in my life that point to wider issues of faith? Reveal them to me, please.

Inviting the Feast

Lord, I repent of operating out of scarcity when You have given me so much. Thank You that You are a God who satisfies. Help me trust You more fully in this area of need . . .

DAY 5

·····························

FASTING

·····························

THERE IS NO
STICKER CHART

You cannot fast as you do today,
hoping to make your voice heard on high.

—Isaiah 58:4

Hold up your index and middle fingers. Now place them on your
wrist. Got a pulse? Then you've got a pride problem. We all do.
Because our nature is broken by sin, our pride is ever proclaiming that
life is all about us, not about the One who made us. This pride problem
wiggles its way into every corner of our lives, even into our spiritual
disciplines.

Pride convinces us we're superior if we embrace regular rhythms of
fasting. A master at comparison, pride nudges us to notice all of the
other Christ followers who don't. Pride gives us imaginations of a
cosmic sticker chart in heaven, where our commitment to deprivation
earns us gold stars with the Lord. Our pride convinces us that fasting is
about what goes into our mouths. The Bible says, "Not so fast." (Wink.
See what I did there?) It's what comes out of our mouths that counts.

READ ISAIAH 58:1-12.

As we seek to understand what God's Word teaches about fasting and feasting, this passage is as elementary as our ABCs. Notice verse 2, "They seek me day after day and delight to know my ways, like a nation that does what is right and does not abandon the justice of their God. They ask me for righteous judgements; they delight in the nearness of God."

Sounds like a full sticker chart to me! Except it wasn't. The children of Israel were fasting with wrong motives. Skipping meals doesn't permit us to skip out on living lives set apart by the commandments of God.

As I studied this passage, I scribbled two columns on a sheet of lined paper. In column one I listed the criteria for the fast God accepts. (We'll come back to that.) Column two was designated for the characteristics of a fast He doesn't:

- We do as we please on the day of our fast (v. 3).
- We oppress our workers (v. 3).
- And fast with contention, strife, and raised fists (v. 4).

As I read these words, pride tells me I'm doing okay. I can't remember a time I punched someone's lights out during a fast. (Though to be honest, when my blood sugar crashes, I am often tempted to.)

Column one is a longer list because the fast God accepts is much harder to achieve. An acceptable fast means we:

- Deny ourselves (v. 5).
- Take a posture of humility, acknowledging our need (v. 5).
- Lament over our sin (v. 5).
- Break the chains of wickedness (v. 6).
- Set the oppressed free (v. 6).

- Share our bread with the hungry (v. 7).
- Bring the homeless into our homes (v. 7).
- Clothe our naked neighbor (v. 7).
- Be attentive to our family (v. 7).
- Get rid of the finger pointing (v. 9).
- Speak life-giving words to those within earshot (v. 9).

If my pride is an inflated balloon, God's Word is a needle. Pop! Suddenly I see that I've never fasted like this. In fact, I cannot offer the fast the Lord accepts without the Spirit's help.

Food is never mentioned in this foundational fasting passage because fasting isn't about food; it's about faithfulness. Fasting is an opportunity to celebrate God's faithfulness to us and His commitment to fully transform us. Fasting is just one way we can express our commitment to live like He calls us to live.

There are no sticker charts in heaven, just sinners redeemed by grace. The gospel is the antidote we desperately need to push back against the poison of pride. What happens when we offer Christ our hearts instead of our food habits?

> The LORD will always lead you,
> satisfy you in a parched land,
> and strengthen your bones.
> You will be like a watered garden
> and like a spring whose water never runs dry. (v. 11)

SETTING THE TABLE, INVITING THE FEAST

*Use the prayer prompts below to ask the Lord
to do an abundant work in your life.*

Setting the Table

*Lord, as I read about the unacceptable fast the nation of Israel
offered You in Isaiah 58, I am convicted that I try to earn your
acceptance by . . .*

_____

_____

_____

_____

_____

_____

_____

_____

_____

_____

_____

_____

_____

_____

_____

Inviting the Feast

Jesus, thank You that because of Your sacrifice, I am fully accepted by the Father. Help me live in the reality of the love the Father has freely poured out on me in You instead of trying to earn His love.

FEASTING

NOT THE KALE OF LIFE

"I am the bread of life," Jesus told them. "No one who comes to me will ever be hungry, and no one who believes in me will ever be thirsty again."

—John 6:35

In the wee hours of the morning, as the sun begins to rise over the little farm where I live, you can find me blending. I start most mornings by gulping down a green smoothie. Though I am a believer in the health benefits that come from kick-starting my day with a bunch of fresh greens, this ritual is primarily rewarding, rarely satisfying.

READ JOHN 6:22–42.

These verses describe the morning after the feeding of the five thousand. Though the miracle was still fresh on the minds of the people who had witnessed it, their bellies had begun to rumble again. They wanted more from Jesus. "What can we do to perform the works of God?," they wondered out loud (v. 28).

Ever wish you could perfectly recreate Olive Garden breadsticks in your own kitchen? Or produce the salsa from your favorite Mexican restaurant with tomatoes from your backyard garden? The crowds that had been miraculously fed wished the same thing was possible for their spiritual cravings.

They were essentially asking, "How can we whip up our own miracle bread at home, without You, Jesus?" It's a question our hearts repeat as often as I blend a smoothie. Our sin nature creates a gravitational pull toward anything that holds the promise of satisfaction. I feel this pull daily in relationship with food. Maybe a new water bottle will transform how I feel. Maybe I need more fruit. Maybe I need less fruit. Maybe some new recipes will satisfy my hunger. Maybe eating out tonight will.

And while moving toward most things on my long list of cravings usually provides some temporary reward, they can never satisfy me for long or curb my deepest, most desperate yearnings. This reality is what Jesus was addressing in John 6:35.

> "I am the bread of life," Jesus told them. "No one who comes to me will ever be hungry, and no one who believes in me will ever be thirsty again."

Though the crowd seemed to crave it, Jesus didn't pass along His divine bread recipe. He didn't deliver an unlimited supply of multiplying loaves and fishes. Instead He offered Himself. The crowd wondered if Jesus was enough (vv. 41–42). Feel familiar?

Our physical cravings are real. They require real food. But aren't they also reminders that we tend to crave what can never fill us? And that Jesus makes it possible to be satiated in the hungriest parts of our souls?

Why didn't He describe Himself as the Kale of Life? He made every cell in our bodies. He knows what we need most, but He's not the Omega Fatty Acid of Life or the Superfood of Life. He is the Bread of Life. He satisfies our cravings in a way nothing else ever can. **Daily bread is a daily reminder that full vitality and full contentment are fully found in Him.**

Are you holding your nose and powering through your relationship with Jesus? In your mind, is your faith mostly built on *shoulds* and *have-tos*? Or do you enjoy Him? Do you believe with every cell He's made in you that He enjoys you?

Pastor John Piper describes his philosophy of the Christian life this way: "God is glorified most not by merely being known, nor by merely being dutifully obeyed, but by being enjoyed in the knowing and in the obeying."[1] In other words, "God is most glorified in us when we are most satisfied in Him."[2]

I nod to the power of my morning green smoothie, but I've dedicated my life to the Bread of Life. The message the hungry crowds missed was that He doesn't offer us spiritual health at the cost of full satisfaction. He is able to meet our needs *and* satisfy our longings. *He gives us life and life abundant.*

Here's a question to sit with today: Is Christ being glorified because you are so satisfied in Him?

SETTING THE TABLE, INVITING THE FEAST

*Use the prayer prompts below to ask the Lord
to do an abundant work in your life.*

Setting the Table

*Jesus, I am like the crowd described in John 6, always craving
solutions that can never fully satisfy. I see this pattern most clearly
in my relationship with food in my tendency to . . .*

_____

_____

_____

_____

_____

Inviting the Feast

*Lord, teach me how to have a relationship with food that fully
satisfies my body. More importantly, teach me how to have a
relationship with You that fully satisfies my craving for . . .*

_____

_____

_____

_____

_____

_____

_____

BAD FRUIT

*Now the works of the flesh are obvious: sexual immorality, moral
impurity, promiscuity, idolatry, sorcery, hatreds, strife, jealousy,
outbursts of anger, selfish ambition, dissensions, factions, envy,
drunkenness, carousing, and anything similar. I am warning
you about these things—as I warned you before—that those who
practice such things will not inherit the kingdom of God.*

—Galatians 5:19–21

Did you skim through the passage above wondering what in the
world these verses have to do with food? Feels a little heavy-
handed to drop "sorcery" and "outbursts of anger" into a devotional
about fasting and feasting, doesn't it? Except, this is more than a list of
behaviors best avoided. It's a list of fruit—rotten fruit.

You may be more familiar with the second grocery list found in
Galatians 6, the fruit of the Spirit. It's a notable list of gifts given to
every follower of Christ. But the flesh produces fruit, too. It's the kind
of fruit best thrown out.

READ GALATIANS 5:16-21.

Several years ago I was teaching at a women's conference, and I invited the women in the room to write down the areas of sin they struggled with most. I was shocked by their answers but not because they confessed to "shocking" sins. What raised my eyebrows and hurt my heart was that the area of "sin" mentioned most often was food. Over and over women poured out their hearts on tear-stained pages about their battle with food. Though I can empathize with the angst, we've got a bigger problem than whether we can resist a third (okay fourth) slice of pizza: **we don't seem to grasp what sin is.**

The genesis of sin is found in the book of Genesis. When Adam and Eve distorted the words of God, cooperated with the enemy of God, and disobeyed the command of God, they sinned. When we repeat the pattern, we sin too.

Sin is, and always has been, a violation of God's Word.

- Sin is not guilt that you ate too many cookies.
- Sin is not shame that you like your popcorn with extra butter.
- Sin is not fear that God is mad at you because you drink your coffee with full-fat creamer.

Sin is more serious than the calories we put into our mouths. *Sin doesn't grow in our stomachs. It grows in our hearts.*

I am the pot calling the kettle black here. I fixate on trouble spots that God never does. I weep over my battle with food and weight and downplay the devastation caused by my sin. I feel ashamed of what I put on my plate and excuse what comes out of my mouth. I bear a heavy weight of guilt over the numbers on the scale but don't bear with my brothers and sisters in Christian love. I fret over habits with no eternal significance and ignore the stench of the rotten fruit of my flesh. I have a hunch your head is nodding and your heart is crying, "Me too."

This is the same bait and switch the enemy deployed in the garden. He distracted Adam and Eve with a shiny piece of fruit, and suddenly they forgot what God said or why it mattered. The forbidden fruit was never the real problem. It is fruit of the flesh that wreaks real havoc in our world. Yet for every moment of misplaced sorrow, there is a handle of truth to hold on to: if we are in Christ, the Holy Spirit is at work within us replacing the bad fruit of the flesh with the good fruit of the Spirit.

You may have real issues related to your relationship with food. This may be an area where the Lord intends to put you on His anvil to stretch and shape you more into His image. But ultimately, the issue is not the food itself. Rebellion lives first in our hearts, not our hands. **Instead of focusing on the fruit in our fridge, we need the Spirit's help to consider the fruit in our lives.**

As you continue to look at fasting and feasting through the lens of God's Word, let these questions recalibrate your vision:

- Do I know what sin is?
- Do I weep over evidence of the fruit of the flesh in my life as often or as passionately as I weep over my frustration with food?
- Have I fallen for the original bait and switch, fixating on physical cravings while ignoring the sinful cravings of my flesh?

SETTING THE TABLE, INVITING THE FEAST

Use the prayer prompts below to ask the Lord
to do an abundant work in your life.

Setting the Table

Jesus, left to my own devices, I will convince myself that the sin
of the flesh is what is best for me and the fruit of the Spirit is
something I can live without. Help me agree with You on what
matters most and remember that sin is . . .

_____

_____

_____

_____

_____

_____

_____

_____

_____

_____

_____

_____

_____

_____

Inviting the Feast

Lord, is there evidence of the fruit of the flesh in my life? If so, expose it and help me repent.

Pray through Galatians 5:16–21 and write down any areas of conviction.

_____

_____

_____

_____

_____

_____

_____

_____

_____

_____

_____

_____

_____

_____

_____

_____

_____

_____

_____

FEASTING

THE TIGER IN A BOX

Give us today our daily bread.

—Matthew 6:11

An image of his bearded face probably hangs on one of the walls of your childhood. It certainly hangs in mine. Taken in 1918, *Grace* is the official title given to the photograph that eventually became a painting and went on to become one of the most replicated prints of all time. You can probably close your eyes and picture the white-headed man in the photo: his face creased with deep wrinkles, his table adorned with simple food and a big book, his hands clasped in prayer.

The photo was taken by Eric Enstrom when a foot-scraper salesman (the old man in the photo) stopped by Enstrom's little Minnesota studio. As the world endured the endless sorrows of World War I, Enstrom began to circulate his photo as his way of reminding his brethren that thankfulness lights our path to hope.

"I wanted to take a picture that would show people that even though they had to do without many things because of the war they still had much to be thankful for."[3]

Why are we hungry so often? Sharks can live without food for ten weeks. Cave-dwelling olms can survive a decade without food.[4] Yet our bellies rumble every few hours. Why did God create us with this built-in need meter? Why must the alarm go off so often?

READ MATTHEW 6:11.

I once heard our relationship with food described as a tiger in a box. Three times a day we take the tiger out and feed him. As we attempt to contain our cravings day after day, year after year, sometimes the tiger bites back.

You wake up every morning, and the tiger growls for breakfast. At lunchtime he bares his teeth again. His low growl can be heard at dinner. If you don't feed the tiger, he will get louder and louder. This daily reminder of our physical needs is an inescapable reality. Every man, woman, and child are united by our constant need for food.

This daily struggle is ultimately a lavish grace because daily hunger is one of many ways God alerts us to our desperate need for Him.

I've heard it said this way: anything is a blessing that makes us pray. In other words, any pang that makes us aware of our desperate need is a gift.

Without hunger we'd all convince ourselves that we don't need anyone or anything. "I'm in charge of my destiny!" our flesh screams, but first, "I need a snack." Self-sufficiency is the real tiger, ever purring with the lie that we can take care of ourselves. Except, of course, we can't. We need food. We need water. We need love and compassion and purpose. We need redemption. We need hope. We need peace. Because we cannot meet these needs on our own, they are reminders of just how desperately we need a Savior—and just how much He wants to meet those needs.

Perhaps the *Grace* painting arrests our hearts because it captures an old man at the moment God responded to his need alarm. It was the moment he put the tiger back in the box with simple thanks.

Every grace-filled reminder of our insufficiency points our hearts back to our sufficient Savior. Every pang is a reminder He is near, He wants to satisfy us, and He is not surprised by the new needs we bring in hand as we come to Him. He would not install an alarm to remind you of your needs if He did not desire to meet those needs! When hunger strikes today, you have two options: thank the Lord for His reminder that you need Him or try to meet the need in your own strength. Choose the former. Fold your hands. Close your eyes. Give thanks that God has reminded you of your desperate need—what grace!

SETTING THE TABLE, INVITING THE FEAST

*Use the prayer prompts below to ask the Lord
to do an abundant work in your life.*

_____

Setting the Table

*Jesus, thank You for daily reminders that I need You. Today those
reminders came in the form of . . .*

_____

_____

_____

_____

_____

_____

Inviting the Feast

*Lord, teach me to resist my inclination toward self-sufficiency. Help
me run to You with my needs, even now. I confess I have been
ignoring my need alarm in the area of . . .*

_____

_____

_____

_____

_____

_____

_____

....

FASTING

....

SIDE-BY-SIDE SACRIFICE

*As they were worshiping the Lord and fasting, the Holy
Spirit said, "Set apart for me Barnabas and Saul for the
work to which I have called them." Then after they had fasted,
prayed, and laid hands on them, they sent them off."*

—Acts 13:2–3

Pull out your mental scrapbook. In your mind, flip through the
images of your most cherished memories from your walk with
Jesus. I'm going to make an assumption based on my own experiences:
you're not the only one in each frame.

Perhaps, like me, you were surrounded by other teenagers in a hot
auditorium on the night you surrendered your life to Christ. Maybe
close friends and family stood on a muddy riverbank as you followed
Jesus' example through believer's baptism. Can you picture hands lifted
in praise in your periphery as you reflect on your most meaningful
moments of worship? Maybe your best memories include the circle of
smiling faces that make up your weekly Bible study group.

While faith is certainly personal, it is rarely private. It's communal.
The Word encourages us to do most of the activity of the Christian life

together, including fasting. God's work in our lives and in our world is like a big bowl of buttered popcorn that we get to pass and share.

READ ACTS 13:1–3.

Make a quick list of who was gathered together in the church at Antioch (v. 1).

_____

_____

_____

Lest you read these words and picture a polite prayer gathering in a church lobby, skim the preceding chapter of Acts. Persecution against Christ's followers was surging. James had just been executed for his faith (12:2). Peter was on the run from the authorities (12:5–17). The political landscape had destabilized (12:20–29). How did this band of Christian brothers respond? These verses give us a peek into their war room. The weapon they deployed was the three-pronged spear of prayer, fasting, and community.

As we consider what God's Word says about fasting, this story is just one strand of a cord woven throughout both Testaments.

- The whole nation of Israel fasted for a day in response to their corporate sin in the book of 1 Samuel (7:5–6).
- Esther asked all of the Jews in Susa to fast for three days before she boldly approached King Ahasuerus to plead for their lives (Esther 4:15–17).
- The whole nation of Nineveh fasted after Jonah prophesied God's coming judgment (Jonah 3:5–10).

Scripture makes a compelling case for corporate fasting to be the norm, not the exception.

- I know of a pastor in Pennsylvania who calls his entire congregation to fast for twenty-one days at the turn of every new year.
- I'm friends with families who have fasted together when facing moments of great financial or relational need.
- I've heard political leaders call for widespread fasting during times of national crisis.

Let these examples marinate for a while and picture your mental scrapbook once again. Imagine what new pictures God could glue into ~~yours~~. Scratch that—into *ours*.

- Picture victories in our marriages as we fast and pray together.
- Picture revival in our churches as congregations commit to seek the Lord with renewed passion together.
- Picture transformed nations who, like the Ninevites, fast to turn to the Lord in repentance together.
- Picture women on every continent wielding the three-pronged sword of prayer, fasting, and togetherness.

To be clear, Scripture does not indicate that more people fasting produces different results than a single person fasting. As we're learning, the goal of fasting is not to manipulate God into jumping through our hoops. The power of corporate fasting is solidarity. As Paul and the church leaders sequestered at Antioch to fast and pray, they were saying with their actions, "We are in this together. We will stand tall for Jesus, side by side."

SETTING THE TABLE, INVITING THE FEAST

*Use the prayer prompts below to ask the Lord
to do an abundant work in your life.*

_____

Setting the Table

*Lord, thank You for giving me saints to surround me as I walk in
faith. I'm especially grateful for the ways Christian community
strengthens me in the area of . . .*

_____

_____

_____

_____

_____

_____

_____

_____

_____

_____

_____

_____

_____

_____

_____

_____

_____

Inviting the Feast

Lord, please give me some creative ideas for how I can use the three-pronged spear of prayer, fasting, and community more effectively.

Write down whatever comes to mind.

_____

_____

_____

_____

_____

_____

_____

_____

_____

_____

_____

_____

_____

_____

_____

_____

_____

_____

_____

FEASTING

SEVEN FEASTS

The LORD spoke to Moses saying, "Speak to the people of Israel and say to them, These are the appointed feasts of the LORD that you shall proclaim as holy convocations; they are my appointed feasts."

—Leviticus 23:1–2 ESV

READ LEVITICUS 23.

My family and I have an ongoing obsession with survival shows. One of our favorites takes ten survival experts and drops them off at individual sites in the wilderness to fend for themselves. Whoever lasts the longest without store-bought food and tap water, the comforts of home, and connections with other people wins.

Most players make it two to three weeks. The winners hang in there for two to three months. Upon their rescue, they all want the same thing: to enjoy a good meal with the people they love.

The Israelites can surely empathize.

The book of Leviticus finds God's people newly emancipated from the bonds of slavery in Egypt. They didn't know how to live without taskmasters, so God gave them guidelines through the prophet Moses. I wouldn't dare try to edit the Bible, but an accurate subtitle for the book of Leviticus could be "Rules for Wandering." God graciously outlined how the Israelites could flourish as they meandered toward the land He had promised.

In Leviticus 23, God gives the Israelites seven celebrations or "feasts" to observe each year. The seven feasts are a sliver of Scripture as rich as flourless chocolate cake. They point to the gospel, but more practically for the Israelites, they are a clear invitation to enjoy a good meal with the people they love. Many of the feasts involved food, grain, and drink offerings (v. 37). Several involved instructions about what to eat:

- The Passover kicked off the year with roasted lamb, unleavened bread, and bitter herbs (Lev. 23:5; cf. Exod. 12:1–15).
- The Feast of Unleavened Bread required God's children to eat unleavened bread for seven days (Lev. 23:6).
- The Feast of Firstfruits celebrated the harvest with bread and roasted grain (Lev. 23:14).

As I read about the feasts, I am struck anew that God doesn't just teach us how to feed and care for the spiritual man. He lovingly shows us how to care for the physical man (and woman), too.

Though the feasts were deeply spiritual, they were also highly practical. God was giving His people rhythms to remind them of His character. In some ways He was also shaping their relationship with food by teaching them patterns of fasting and feasting.

Wise theologian A. W. Tozer once wrote, "What comes into our minds when we think about God is the most important thing about us."[5]

Pause for a moment and consider: What comes into your mind when you think of God and food? Do you think of Him as unconcerned about what you eat because He is too focused on "more important" things? Scripture begs to differ. Do you imagine He separates the rhythms of your day into "spiritual" and "not so much"? If so, does that align with what you read in His book?

As New Testament believers, the seven feasts don't anchor our rhythms in the same way they did for the Israelites, but *the feasts still matter because they still teach us about the character of God.* He is a God who cares about every part of us, a God who desires to permeate every area of our lives. As the One who designed us, He alone knows the keys to our thriving. Food must be a part of that equation as He mentions it so often in His Word.

In so many ways, we're all wandering. Though as His children we've been set free from the taskmasters of sin and death, we haven't yet arrived in the land He has promised. We don't always know how to flourish in this desert of brokenness.

Yes, we must feed our spirit. We need the disciplines of prayer, worship, and soaking in His Word. But when God was teaching the Israelites how to live, He taught them how to feast. Leviticus 23 is just one of many spots in Scripture that highlight that God cares about the rhythms of our days, our weeks, our months, and our years, including our food rhythms. Chew on that for a moment and consider: Have you invited God into the food rhythms of your life? Does your prayer life steer clear of the practical areas of your life because you assume God is unconcerned? The rules for wandering are essentially this: lean on God, listen, and obey His voice. As you wander today, ask Him to show you what it means to truly feast.

SETTING THE TABLE, INVITING THE FEAST

*Use the prayer prompts below to ask the Lord
to do an abundant work in your life.*

Setting the Table

God, what comes to mind when I think about You and food is . . .

_____

_____

_____

_____

_____

_____

_____

_____

_____

_____

_____

_____

_____

_____

_____

_____

_____

Inviting the Feast

Lord, I invite You into the food rhythms of my life today. Would You teach me to have a relationship with food that leads to thriving? Would You reveal any eating habits You'd like me to adopt so that I might remember Your character throughout my days and weeks and months? Specifically, I want to learn how to . . .

_____

_____

_____

_____

_____

_____

_____

_____

_____

_____

_____

_____

_____

_____

_____

_____

_____

_____

_____

_____

_____

FASTING TO REPENT

*Then the people of Nineveh believed God. They proclaimed a fast
and dressed in sackcloth—from the greatest of them to the least.*

—Jonah 3:5

When we retell the story of Jonah in our colorful children's Bibles and Sunday school classrooms, we typically focus on what the great fish ate—Jonah, the guy the book is named after. The real heartbeat of the story centers on what the Ninevites ate. More specifically, why they chose not to eat at all.

The book of Jonah is famous for good reason. With a runaway prophet, a man-swallowing fish, and a prophetic message of impending judgment, it is a real page-turner. But the narratives found in Scripture are so much more than good bedtime stories. Each one has something to teach us about the character of God and how He calls us to live.

READ JONAH 3.

Jonah's whole "adventure" began when "the word of the LORD came to Jonah son of Amittai: 'Get up! Go to the great city of Nineveh and preach against it because their evil has come up before me'" (Jonah 1:1–2). God is deadly serious about sin. On the other hand, Jonah took sin (both the Ninevites' and his own) more lightly, resulting in a self-inflicted detour to Nineveh by way of a boat, a storm, and a fish belly.

God has not changed since the days of Jonah. He is still steadfastly committed to ridding our lives of sin. As a holy God, He cannot tolerate it. As a loving Father, He desires us to be free of the disastrous effects of our rebellion. But let's be honest, don't we often respond to our sin and to the sins of others more like Jonah did? We'd rather not confront it. God's judgment makes us uncomfortable. Can't we just take a nice boat ride toward oblivion instead? Jonah's discovery is our reality: we cannot run from the consequences of sin. For truly, "if I go up to heaven, you are there; if I make my bed in Sheol, you are there" (Ps. 139:8).

Sit with the book of Jonah for a while. Consider the contrast. Jonah, God's prophet, was content to let his neighbors perish in their sin. But the Ninevites, a pagan people known for their wicked cruelty, responded altogether differently.

> Now Nineveh was an extremely great city, a three-day walk. Jonah set out on the first day of his walk in the city and proclaimed, "In forty days Nineveh will be demolished!" Then the people of Nineveh believed God. *They proclaimed a fast and dressed in sackcloth—from the greatest of them to the least.* (Jonah 3:3–6, emphasis added)

Nearly as soon as Jonah's sandals hit their city streets with a call to repentance, the Ninevites declared a fast. Fasting can never force God's forgiveness. He gives it freely to all who are willing to turn from their sin (1 John 1:9). But like so many other parts of the Christian life, fasting is an outward expression of inward heart change. Fasting is one way we can express that we agree with God on the seriousness of sin and we are sorry for violating His perfect law.

God's people have been fasting as a sign of repentance for millennia.

- The book of Nehemiah tells us that the entire nation of Israel fasted in repentance before resettling in Jerusalem (9:1–4).
- Through the prophet Joel, God declared, "Even now . . . turn to me with all your heart, with fasting, weeping, and mourning. Tear your hearts, not just your clothes, and return to the LORD your God" (2:12–13).
- First Samuel 7 tells us that God's people poured out water before the Lord as an expression of what God was doing in their hearts, and they fasted collectively because of their sin (v. 6).
- Even wicked King Ahab fasted when the prophet Elijah pointed out his unrighteousness. Scripture tells us that because of Ahab's expression of humility, expressed through fasting, God delayed His judgment for a generation (1 Kings 21:29).

Perhaps you're still wrestling with the concept of fasting. You're still wondering if it's for you. Here's a bottom-line question: Are you a sinner? The answer is yes, of course. Here's a follow-up: Are you grieved by your own sin, the sin of someone you love, or of the nation you live in? Scripture gives us a precedent for how to respond—we fast. Fasting in repentance is a way we can live set apart. It is external evidence of the internal work God is doing as He transforms us from sinners to saints.

Can you repent without fasting? Of course. This isn't a mandate. But consider the book of Jonah once more. Whose example do you most want to emulate? The self-righteous prophet who responded to his neighbor's sin with self-protection? (How'd that work out, Jonah?) Or the Ninevites who, once confronted with the reality of their sinfulness, expressed genuine repentance through fasting?

SETTING THE TABLE, INVITING THE FEAST

*Use the prayer prompts below to ask the Lord
to do an abundant work in your life.*

Setting the Table

*Jesus, like Jonah, I am uncomfortable confronting my sin and the
sins of others because . . .*

_____

_____

_____

_____

_____

_____

_____

_____

_____

_____

_____

_____

_____

_____

_____

_____

_____

Inviting the Feast

Lord, what are some ways I can outwardly express my inward desire to turn from sin?

Write or draw whatever comes to mind.

_____

_____

_____

_____

_____

_____

_____

_____

_____

_____

_____

_____

_____

_____

_____

_____

_____

_____

_____

_____

_____

_____

_____

_____

FEASTING

THE MINISTRY OF PANCAKES

Jesus said to them, "Come and have breakfast." Now none of the disciples dared ask him, "Who are you?" They knew it was the Lord.

—John 21:12 ESV

I was nine months pregnant with my second child when a plate of pancakes saved my life. If that sounds dramatic, perhaps you've not experienced (or forgotten the reality of) carrying an eight-pound baby inside your body, while a twenty-five-pound toddler constantly clings to the outside of your body. I needed a nap. I needed a friend. I needed a heavy dose of hope and perspective. I found all three in a perfectly prepared stack of buttermilk pancakes.

Mandy and I were acquaintances at church, just familiar enough to wave sheepishly if we saw each other in the grocery store. So imagine my surprise when Mandy called me late one evening and said, "Come over in the morning with Eli." (Eli is my firstborn.) "Stay in your jammies. I will make you breakfast."

Though I'm ordinarily not the kind of woman who moseys over to the home of an acquaintance with my hair unbrushed and my child still wearing his overnight diaper, the invitation was so irresistible, I complied. The next morning, there we stood on Mandy's stoop. Unkempt and unpretentious, longing to be fed.

As Eli played on the floor, Mandy served me a plate of buttery pancakes. It was one of most significant meals I've ever eaten. Every bite preached a sermon to my weary heart:

- You are seen.
- You are beloved.
- You have been commissioned for this assignment.
- Jesus has not abandoned you.

It's not like Mandy opened her Bible and read Scripture over me. She simply gave me the ministry of her presence, and I have a hunch, all these years later, that she prayed for my heart to be strengthened as she watched me take each bite.

In John 21, we find Jesus loving others well with the gift of a hot breakfast.

READ JOHN 21:11–14.

This chapter of Scripture represents every moment of despair, defeat, discouragement, or disappointment we've ever felt. The preceding verses describe the most significant and hope-filled event in history, the resurrection of Jesus Christ. Sin and death had been conquered, and yet our broken planet kept spinning on its tilted axis. Jesus has saved us! We have true, transformative hope in Him. Yet we remain broken people traversing a broken planet. Our lives have aches and pains that range from the obnoxious to the overwhelming. John 21 displays the tenderness with which Jesus responds to our chronic state of need.

The resurrected Savior had appeared to His disciples as they hid behind the false security of locked doors, but He didn't stay with them. They knew Jesus had been crucified. They knew He had risen, but everything else about their lives was shrouded in mystery. Would He establish His kingdom on the earth? Would He take them with Him to be in glory? Would they see Him again soon? Were they safe? Was He pleased? What were they supposed to do now?

The disciples used a coping mechanism I've used often myself; overwhelmed by all they didn't know, they stuck to the familiar. They went fishing. I imagine they dropped anchor in their favorite fishing hole and cast their nets in hope that their proven patterns of success would not fail them.

> But that night they caught nothing. (v. 3)

It was insult added to injury, salt poured into their gaping wounds. But Jesus was already stoking the fires of redemption on the shore.

> When they got out on land, they saw a charcoal fire
> in place, with fish laid out on it, and bread. (v. 9)

Jesus helped His friends catch the fish they were after (v. 6), but clearly, He didn't need the contents of their nets. He already had fish starting to sizzle beside a loaf of freshly baked bread. This is a rich passage. There are many important themes worth meditating on, but let's not miss the significance of this simple fact: when Jesus' friends were hurting, He cooked them breakfast. Though still reeling from the disorienting whiplash of the arrest, death, burial, and resurrection of their Savior, this moment was surely a respite. As that warm food hit their grumbling bellies, they must have felt:

- Seen
- Beloved
- Commissioned

Good food was their reminder: Jesus has not abandoned us.

Jesus may not cook your breakfast this morning, but He is offering you the gift of His presence, which is its own sort of daily bread. Jesus deserves the glory for the food on our plates and the freedom of our souls. Every bite of food you will ever eat has been gifted to you by the kind of Savior who goes to the cross for sinners and cooks breakfast for downtrodden friends.

You are free to face your day with the confidence that comes from knowing that Jesus is attentive to your every need: your spiritual needs, your physical needs, your emotional needs, your relational needs. . . . Jesus does not force rank.

Do you want to be like Jesus today? Perhaps it's not as complicated as you think. Turn toward someone who needs Christ-infused hope today—your family, your neighbor, that tired momma you know from church—and repeat after Jesus, "Come and have breakfast" (v. 12).

SETTING THE TABLE, INVITING THE FEAST

*Use the prayer prompts below to ask the Lord
to do an abundant work in your life.*

Setting the Table

*Jesus, as I consider Your Word, I am grateful for all the ways You
comfort me. Today, I am especially thankful for Your comfort in
these situations . . .*

Inviting the Feast

Lord, show me who I can pass Your gift of comfort on to today. Whom should I extend a breakfast invitation to?

_____

_____

_____

_____

_____

_____

_____

_____

_____

_____

_____

_____

_____

_____

_____

_____

_____

_____

_____

_____

_____

_____

FASTING

FASTING FOR REVIVAL

Ezra then went from the house of God and walked to the
chamber of Jehohanan son of Eliashib, where he spent
the night. He did not eat food or drink water, because he
was mourning over the unfaithfulness of the exiles.

—Ezra 10:6

When was the last time you wept over someone else's sin? Has it been days? Years? Decades since tears rolled down your cheeks because other people's rebellion has offended the holy God? Has your heart ever been stricken with true grief over the sins of our culture? Of our world?

While the Ninevites fasted in response to their own grief, Scripture gives us another compelling reason to fast—we fast to demonstrate our grief for the sins of others.

The book of Ezra is a book about revival. After a brutal period of captivity as a result of their sin, God's people were allowed to return home. Yes, they returned physically home to Jerusalem, but through the prophet Ezra and the recovery of the Scriptures, they were invited to a deeper homecoming, to return home to unbroken fellowship with God.

READ EZRA 9–10.

Revival often involves grief. We must face the sin that separated us from God in the first place. For the Israelites in Ezra's day, this included violating His command not to marry people who worshipped other gods from neighboring nations. (In the time of Ezra, marriage with someone from another nation was deemed sinful not because the two came from different countries but because they worshipped different gods. To marry a woman from another nation typically resulted in taking on whatever god her nation worshipped.) They disobeyed and, as warned, turned from God's perfect law as a result.

Ezra's response to the people's rebellion is a picture of how sin should affect us all: "When I heard this report, I tore my tunic and robe, pulled out some of the hair from my head and beard, and sat down devastated" (v. 9:3).

Ezra had not personally married a woman from the nations God warned him not to. He was devastated by the sins of his countrymen, laid flat by his fellow heirs to the promises of God. Look again at his response. Notice that he didn't politely suppress a lump in his throat. His was clothes-tearing, beard-plucking, sit-you-down-in-the-dirt, visceral grief. It was a grief that led to fasting.

I don't know what nation you live in, but chances are, I don't need to list off the sins of that nation to you. You already know them. The stench of the sin around us sticks to us like bonfire smoke. We are prone to respond with exasperation, disgust, and/or turning a blind eye. The Bible gives us an alternative: grief-fueled fasting.

As I read Ezra 9 and 10, I am not surprised God's people—even the sons of the priests!—rebelled. We've been doing that since the garden of Eden. I'm not surprised God called His children back to Him. He's been doing that since the fall. What jumps off the page at me are the words of Shecaniah son of Jaheil, the Elamite: "We have been unfaithful to our God by marrying foreign women from the surrounding peoples, but there is still hope for Israel in spite of this. . . . Get up, for this matter is your responsibility, and we support you. Be strong and take action!" (10:2, 4).

What a moment. What a speech!

So, what action did Ezra take in response?

> He did not eat food or drink water, because he
> was mourning over the unfaithfulness of the exiles.
> (10:6)

Add this to the growing list of reasons Scripture invites us to fast—we fast in grief for the sins of others. This kind of fast is both an expression of the depth of our sorrow over sin and a means to cry out to the Lord for true and widespread revival.

Does it work? Can fasting for the sins of those still running from God in glad rebellion really make a difference?

Ask the priests. We find the names of their descendants listed right alongside everyone else who was guilty of unfaithfulness to God (10:18–43). God used Ezra's grief and his fasting to change their hearts: "They pledged to send their wives away, and being guilty, they offered a ram from the flock for their guilt" (10:19). Where they once made room for other false gods, they now turned their heart back to the one true God. What fruit from fasting!

SETTING THE TABLE, INVITING THE FEAST

*Use the prayer prompts below to ask the Lord
to do an abundant work in your life.*

Setting the Table

*God, give me true, righteous grief over the sins of others. Today I
cry out for revival for those caught in unfaithfulness to You. I beg
You to turn their hearts from other gods to You, the one true God. I
ask You to set them free from the false gods of . . .*

_____

_____

_____

_____

_____

_____

_____

_____

_____

_____

_____

_____

_____

_____

_____

Inviting the Feast

Lord, show me good ways I can take action to respond rightly to other people's sins. Give me ideas for how I might develop a rhythm of fasting to intercede for revival.

Write or draw whatever comes to mind.

_____

_____

_____

_____

_____

_____

_____

_____

_____

_____

_____

_____

_____

_____

_____

_____

_____

_____

_____

FEASTING

EAT THE RASPBERRIES

Here is what I have seen to be good: It is appropriate to eat, drink, and experience good in all the labor one does under the sun during the few days of his life God has given him, because that is his reward.

—Ecclesiastes 5:18

I have a bizarre relationship with raspberries.

Several times a year, I put a package or two of fresh raspberries in my shopping cart as a reward. I adore raspberries. They feel like an indulgent departure from the everyday fruits that typically fill my fruit bowl: grapes, apples, and bananas. Here's the weird part: nine times out of ten, I let the raspberries rot. The luscious treat turns from deep pink to fuzzy green before I throw them out and repeat the cycle.

I can't write a book for women about food without touching on the subject of shame. Perhaps it is because our foremother Eve sinned by eating forbidden fruit. Maybe it's a by-product of a marketing culture determined to separate us from our money by convincing us of a felt need. It's probably a combination of both. For most of us, food and shame go together like peas and carrots.

My rotten raspberries can testify to this; I buy them to treat myself and always decide later that was a silly thing to do. I can never work hard enough or long enough to feel really good about indulging, so the raspberries stay in the fridge. Then I feel dumb about letting them rot. Shame heaps on top of shame to create a pitiful sundae.

READ ECCLESIASTES 5:8–20.

King Solomon knew a thing or two about a thing or two. The whole book of Ecclesiastes is essentially Sociology 101 according to Solomon. Scripture tells us that his insight was great and his understanding was as "vast as the sand on the seashore" (1 Kings 4:29). He observed and recorded what experience taught him to be true about humanity; then he applied the filter of his God-given wisdom.

Solomon's musings about food go against the grain of nearly everything our food-and-diet-obsessed culture has taught us. He wrote, "It is appropriate to eat, drink, and experience good in all the labor one does under the sun during the few days of his life God has given him, because that is his reward" (Eccles. 5:18). Solomon is repeating the invitation to feast that God repeats so often in His Word.

I've read a zillion articles and social media posts telling me I should never reward myself with food. As a result, I feel guilty if I celebrate another year of marriage with a big, juicy steak or a victory at work with a bowl of cookie dough ice cream. But should I? Should you?

Here is a better question: Does shame ever come from the Spirit of God?

To be fair, Solomon didn't always manage his wisdom wisely. We can look at his life and see that overindulgence led to idolatry (1 Kings 11:4) and apply that as a warning to all of God's good and perfect gifts. But Solomon did have one important idea right: God is a God of abundance, not a God of scarcity. He looked around and saw full plates and full bellies as a God-given reward, not a source of God-given shame.

God cares about the details of our lives (including what we eat and don't eat). There may be moments when He challenges us to make wiser food choices for our good. That is in line with His character as a loving and attentive God who designed our bodies to flourish when we take care of them. Ask yourself this: Does the voice that says you are bad for eating something, or you are a failure for struggling with food, or you should deprive yourself to make up for past indulgences line up with the God you find in the pages of your Bible? He is and always will be a God of abundant love, abundant grace, and abundant gifts for His children. The gospel is His profound invitation to stop listening to the voice of shame.

As you think about your own food habits, you must wrestle with the same questions Solomon and I have: Is God a God of scarcity or abundance? Does He primarily want to withhold good from you, or is His desire to give you blessings in abundance? Is He a God who shames His kids into acting the right way or a God who rewards His children with good gifts?

Abundance for you today might look like tapping into the overflowing power you've been given in Christ to turn from food as your god or your first source of comfort. Or it might look like enjoying those raspberries in full freedom or exploring food in a way you've never allowed yourself to experience before. The Holy Spirit leads each of us differently in each moment, but here's the truth: *none of those moments include shame, and all of those moments are fueled by God's never-ending abundance.*

If there are rotten raspberries sitting in your fridge right now or food habits that make you feel like a failure, park your heart on the character of God.

> In place of your shame, you will have a double portion;
> in place of disgrace, they will rejoice over their share.
> So they will possess double in their land,
> and eternal joy will be theirs. (Isa. 61:7)

SETTING THE TABLE, INVITING THE FEAST

*Use the prayer prompts below to ask the Lord
to do an abundant work in your life.*

Setting the Table

*Jesus, as I consider Your Word, I am reminded that You give
abundant gifts to me. I realize I have a scarcity mindset in the area
of . . .*

_____

_____

_____

_____

_____

_____

_____

_____

_____

_____

_____

_____

_____

_____

_____

Inviting the Feast

Lord, I know that shame does not come from You. Set me free from shame in the area of . . .

_____

_____

_____

_____

_____

_____

_____

_____

_____

_____

_____

_____

_____

_____

_____

_____

_____

_____

_____

_____

_____

....

FASTING

....

WHEN AND THEN

And when you fast . . .

—Matthew 6:16 ESV

READ MATTHEW 6:16–18.

Jesus' most famous sermon, the Sermon on the Mount, is recorded in Matthew 5–6. Try to picture Jesus sitting on the hillside with people gathered on every side, eager to learn how to live thriving lives. Christ's practical instructions are secondary in importance to knowing and responding to the gospel, but once we've decided to follow Jesus, the Sermon on the Mount gives us an owner's manual of sorts for how to live set apart, godly lives. In many ways these two chapters of Scripture are the primer for how to live the Christian life.

Immediately following His instructions on how to pray (6:1–15), Jesus gave direction on how to fast. Pay attention to how He began:

"And when you fast . . ."

Pull out your pen. Circle the word "when" in your Bible. Then notice what words aren't present:

- if
- should
- might

Jesus' message about fasting was built on the premise that it was a discipline His followers were already practicing. That little word "when" moves fasting from the fringe to the norm. Though never a command, fasting is an expectation for the follower of Christ.

It may feel like a contradiction, but a few chapters later, in Matthew 9, John's followers asked Jesus why His disciples didn't fast regularly. Jesus replied, "Can the wedding guests be sad while the groom is with them? *The time will come when the groom will be taken away from them, and then they will fast*" (v. 15, emphasis added).

Pull out your pen. Circle the word "then" in your Bible.

Again, Jesus was establishing an expectation. Once He was no longer physically present with His disciples, they would need a different way to pray. *Then*, not *if*, they would become followers who fasted. We could paraphrase Jesus' response to John's disciples this way, "When the time is right—when I leave them and go to my Father—then My people will fast."

According to the time line Jesus gave, the time is right, *right now*.

Let's cut and paste some of our own experiences and desires into Jesus' when/then paradigm.

When we study Jesus' life, then we see that He fasted.

When we read His Word, then we see that fasting is important to Him.

When we fast, then we stand in solidarity with Jesus' disciples and followers who also fast.

And, perhaps most importantly . . .

When we seek to know the heart of God, then we fast out of grateful trust, never blind obligation.

SETTING THE TABLE, INVITING THE FEAST

Use the prayer prompts below to ask the Lord to do an abundant work in your life.

Setting the Table

Jesus, when I consider that You used the words "when" and "then" to describe fasting, it teaches me the following about Your heart toward this discipline in my life . . .

_____

_____

_____

_____

_____

_____

_____

_____

_____

_____

_____

_____

_____

Write down whatever comes to mind.

Inviting the Feast

Lord, sometimes I can misunderstand Your expectations of me as rules I must follow to earn Your love. Instead of hoops I must jump through to be accepted by You, help me understand Your expectations in light of the true gospel. The areas of my life I've been running from Your loving expectations are . . .

FEASTING

THE MARSHMALLOW TEST

For the grace of God has appeared, bringing salvation for all people,
training us to renounce ungodliness and worldly passions, and to
live self-controlled, upright, and godly lives in the present age.

—Titus 2:11–12 ESV

Should you need further proof that God cares about what we eat, Leviticus 11 should do the trick. This is the most detailed list of food laws handed down by God to His people.

READ LEVITICUS 11.

To truly grasp what God wants to teach us through His Word, we look to Scripture to interpret Scripture. Since the Bible tells us that God is good and does good (Ps. 119:68), we can know that He mandated these food laws for the good of the Israelites, but since we're tempted to eat carbs and sugar more often than camels and hyraxes, what do these laws have to teach us about our relationship with food? (As a side note: What is a hyrax?)

Stick a ribbon in Leviticus 11 for a sec. Let's play connect the dots and move to Romans 7. Here's a skosh of background info. Since Paul was born and raised as an orthodox Jew, he would have known and obeyed the Old Testament food laws. Once he had a literal encounter with Jesus (Acts 9), he saw the law through the lens of the gospel. Paul's conversion was a bitter pill for his fellow Jews to swallow. For generations and with great zeal, the Jews depended on their adherence to God's law to redeem them. They worried that Paul was advocating they throw that baby out with the bathwater of blind faith.

Into that tension Paul wrote these words: "What should we say then? Is the law sin? Absolutely not! On the contrary, *I would not have known sin if it were not for the law*" (Rom. 7:7 HCSB, emphasis added).

Though I wasn't there to witness it, I can say with full confidence that God's people did not perfectly keep the food laws He outlined so clearly in Leviticus 11 because they did not perfectly keep the other laws He outlined elsewhere in Scripture. The point Paul is making here is that if God did not tell us His good and right plan for our lives so clearly, we wouldn't have a clue that we violate it so often. God's law is a magnifying glass by which we have eyes to see the true condition of our sinful hearts.

Let's connect another dot. Titus 2 records more of Paul's words. In some ways, this passage is a continuation of his thought process from Romans 7.

> For the grace of God has appeared, bringing salvation for all people, training us to renounce ungodliness and worldly passions, and to live self-controlled, upright, and godly lives in the present age, waiting for our blessed hope, the appearing of the glory of our great God and Savior Jesus Christ, who gave himself for us to redeem us from all lawlessness and

to purify for himself a people for his own possession who are zealous for good works. (Titus 2:11–14 ESV)

There the gospel goes wedging its way into our everyday choices again. Does our approach to food require self-control? You betcha. Can we ever get there with more rules and stricter diet plans? If your experiences mirror mine and the experiences of the Old Testament Israelites, the answer is a big fat no.

I'm sure you've heard of the marshmallow test. Researchers place a marshmallow in front of a small child and tell them not to eat it immediately, promising that if the child waits she will receive two marshmallows. Then the researcher leaves the room. Some children are able to withstand the temptation. But most pop the fluffy puff of sugar in their mouths the instant the adult is out of sight.

Maybe you can resist a literal marshmallow (I prefer mine fire roasted and wedged between two graham crackers and a Reese's peanut butter cup). But apart from the grace of Jesus, none of us live lives governed by self-control. *We're all marshmallow poppers.*

When we apply a rules-based strategy to our approach to food, we will inevitably respond the way God's people did to the list He gave them in Leviticus 11. The rules will feel like a straight jacket, and we will do all we can to wriggle ourselves free. An "eat this, not that" mentality can never work—at least not for long.

The mirror of God's Word reveals that we cannot change ourselves. But grace has accomplished what the rules never could; Jesus *is* making us new. As part of His supernatural work in our hearts and lives through the Holy Spirit who lives in us, He is teaching us to have self-control. The change is happening from the inside out because it can never happen from the outside in. *Ask Him to keep His promise to develop self-control in you as evidence of His profound grace.*

SETTING THE TABLE, INVITING THE FEAST

*Use the prayer prompts below to ask the Lord
to do an abundant work in your life.*

Setting the Table

Jesus, I cannot muster up self-control on my own. I try, but when left to my own devices and strength apart from You, I fail. I see evidence of this reality in these areas of my life . . .

_____

_____

_____

_____

_____

_____

_____

_____

_____

_____

_____

_____

_____

_____

_____

_____

_____

Inviting the Feast

God, as I read Your Word, I see You have promised to teach me to live a self-controlled life and even given me the strength to do so through the power and help of the Holy Spirit. Lord, I see evidence of this truth in these areas of my life . . .

_____

_____

_____

_____

_____

_____

_____

_____

_____

_____

_____

_____

_____

_____

_____

_____

_____

_____

_____

_____

_____

_____

HEART CHECK

Then they said to him, "John's disciples fast often and say prayers,
and those of the Pharisees do the same, but yours eat and drink."

—Luke 5:33

Don't tell me how Big Brother works. I prefer the comfort of my cluelessness. I do know this: as I've been writing a book on fasting and feasting and talking about these concepts more with family and friends, my social media feed has changed. Every day I receive ads promoting the power of fasting for health.

With each sports-bra-clad woman making a promise that fasting is my path to skinny, I am reminded—not all fasting is the same.

READ LUKE 5:33–39.

We've examined this passage already and focused on Jesus' announcement that His disciples would fast when He was no longer physically with them. Let's pick these verses up and look at them from a different angle. Consider: What does this passage tell us about the Pharisees?

Don't overthink it. The answer is as simple as it seems. The Pharisees fasted.

If you've spent much time in the Gospels, you know Jesus often criticized the Pharisees, a group of religiously zealous Jews who had strong opinions about God's law (and voiced those opinions loudly and often).

The Pharisees were not a group of people who denied the existence and importance of God. They were neither atheist nor agnostic. We never find them arguing that God is irrelevant or His law obsolete. Their pendulum swung in the opposite direction. They thought they could earn righteousness and salvation by ticking every religious box.

Over and over in Scripture we see Jesus angry at the Pharisees for doing right things with wrong motives. That M.O. took them so far that they led the charge to kill the world's Savior in the name of protecting God's truth. They were experts at missing the forest for the trees.

This rabbit trail has a lot to teach us about fasting. It's possible to fast consistently and passionately and still miss the reason God invites us to fast in the first place. The Pharisees fasted as a religious ritual. They were just going through the motions. Some likely also fasted as a kind of spiritual flex. If we could read their inner monologue, it would probably sound something like, "I am very, very spiritual. Let me prove it with a fast. A *long* one. Three days longer than Tom's over there! Be impressed."

The ads in my feed display a different version of this by showcasing women fasting to shed pounds. It may work in one sense, but fasting strictly for fitness is another way we can miss the reason God invites us to fast in the first place.

People of other faiths fast, often strictly. Advocates have gone on hunger strikes to express their desperation for societal change. Fasting in itself is not evidence of God's working in us and through us any more than weight loss is evidence of holistic health. Fasting and prayer are two sides of the same divine coin. If you're fasting and not praying, you're just on a diet. If you're fasting and not seeking Jesus, your fasting cannot give you more of Him.

If we don't want to live like the world lives, we cannot fast like the world fasts. Scripture is so kind to warn us that we repeat the Pharisees' mistake when we make sacrifices and miss our Savior.

Following Jesus is heart work. It always will be. When we don't just want fewer calories but, rather, more of Him, we honor the heartbeat of fasting that beats through God's Word. If you are considering the habit of fasting and find yourself a bit fearful of the physical part of the journey, just remember this: it's not even really about checking the box of not eating. It's about making regular room to feast on Jesus. It's not about missing a meal; it's about not missing the Savior.

SETTING THE TABLE, INVITING THE FEAST

*Use the prayer prompts below to ask the Lord
to do an abundant work in your life.*

Setting the Table

*Jesus, sometimes I can get so caught up in doing the "right things"
that I miss the opportunity to seek You. Where am I just going
through the motions of faith without truly seeking Your heart?*

Write down whatever comes to mind.

_____

_____

_____

_____

Inviting the Feast

*Lord, I don't know how to fast in ways that are closer to Scripture
than to the world. Please show me, and give me ideas for how You
might help me take a small step toward the kind of fast You would
have for me in this season.*

Write or draw whatever comes to mind.

_____

_____

_____

_____

_____

FEASTING

SELF-CARE AND SPLINTERS

*Now may the God of peace himself sanctify you completely.
And may your whole spirit, soul, and body be kept sound
and blameless at the coming of our Lord Jesus Christ.*

—1 Thessalonians 5:23

You are a machine, Erin." A friend once made this statement about my drive to work. Though she intended it as a compliment, Satan twisted her words into a sharp splinter and drove them deep into my heart. The splinter soon festered into workaholism and exhaustion. Though I felt the pinch of it, it was in too deep. I didn't know how to pull it out.

The house I grew up in had a long, wooden banister that lined the outdoor stairs. Several times a year I'd run my hand down that banister and implant a splinter into the meat of my hand. My dad would carefully extract each one. It always hurt, but even as a little girl, I understood it was the kind of pain that was necessary for me to be whole and healthy.

God's extraction of our spiritual splinters often works the same way. Over a span of several years, He has removed the lie that I am a machine built to perform as I sat in multiple doctor's offices with questions about chronic pain, unshakable fatigue, and scary symptoms. Every doctor looked at me and said the same thing: "Your body is experiencing too much stress."

Here is the lesson I had to learn the hard way: I am not a disembodied soul. Yes, God has given me a spirit designed to crave Him (Eccles. 3:11). He's commanded me to love Him with my whole heart and mind (Matt. 22:37), but He's also given me a body. This part of us matters to God, too.

READ 1 THESSALONIANS 5:12–28.

Make a list of all of the instructions Paul gives in these verses.

_____   _____
_____   _____
_____   _____
_____   _____
_____   _____
_____   _____
_____   _____
_____   _____
_____   _____
_____   _____
_____   _____
_____   _____

"Comfort the discouraged" (v. 14).

"Rejoice always" (v. 16).

"Hold on to what is good" (v. 21).

These are the exquisite jewels of the Christian life. Paul, in step with the Holy Spirit, was once again telling us how to live set-apart lives, lives that sparkle like emeralds and diamonds in a world of darkness. They are visible, measurable evidence of Christ's profound work in us.

Take out your mental spade and dig a little deeper in verse 23. What parts of the Christian did Paul pray would be kept sound and blameless for the coming of our Lord?

_____

_____

_____

Complete sanctification, complete transformation, complete faith involve the complete person. Circle back to your first list and consider:

- How do you recognize your leaders? With your mouth.
- How do you live at peace with others? With your mouth. With your hands. With your brain. With your heart.
- How do you warn those who are idle? You speak words of truth. You pray prayers of faith. You write words of wisdom. . . .

These are more than ethereal concepts. They are physical extensions of Christ in us. We can comfort the discouraged with a warm meal, prepared with busy hands. We can always rejoice with arms outstretched toward heaven and vocal cords reverberating with songs of praise.

As long as we remain on the earth, we remain inside jars of clay. While it's true that our outer person is decaying now (2 Cor. 4:16), it's also true that our bodies are a God-given gift—so valued by Him, in fact, that He will resurrect them one day!

This reality is part of how God is changing my relationship with food. Eating healthy to fit into a certain pair of jeans puts me in an endless and maddening tug-of-war with food. Eating healthy so that my body is well enough to love and serve others, though—that drops the rope by putting first things first. Self-care as a means of stress reduction usually draws me toward foods that give temporary rewards without any real relief. Self-care as a means of sanctification brings the reward of becoming more like Jesus. Self-care as a way to treat myself feeds my flesh. Self-care as a way to steward what God has given me feeds both my spirit and my body.

Sit still for a moment. Let's take a look at that splinter. Is there evidence that the idea that your body doesn't matter is starting to fester?

Let God's Word minister to your ideas of self-care like a healing balm. May your whole spirit, soul, and body be kept sound and blameless at the coming of our Lord Jesus Christ.

SETTING THE TABLE, INVITING THE FEAST

*Use the prayer prompts below to ask the Lord
to do an abundant work in your life.*

Setting the Table

*Jesus, as I think about my health, I see evidence that I have not
wisely stewarded my body in the fact that I . . .*

_____

_____

_____

_____

_____

_____

_____

_____

_____

_____

_____

_____

_____

_____

_____

_____

_____

_____

Inviting the Feast

Lord, teach me to rightly prioritize my spirit, soul, and body. Pull out any splinters, made from false beliefs about You, that are keeping me from being whole and healthy.

Write down whatever comes to mind.

_____

_____

_____

_____

_____

_____

_____

_____

_____

_____

_____

_____

_____

_____

_____

_____

_____

_____

_____

....

FASTING

....

SELF-DENIAL AND SIMON OF CYRENE

They forced a man coming in from the country,
who was passing by, to carry Jesus's cross.

—Mark 15:21

READ MARK 15:21 AND MATTHEW 16:24–25.

Simon of Cyrene is one of the most blessed men in all of history. The Bible sums up his story in a single sentence, repeated in three of the Gospels.

> They forced a man coming in from the country, who was passing by, to carry Jesus's cross. He was Simon of Cyrene, the father of Alexander and Rufus. (Mark 15:21)

Based on this quick snapshot into his life, it seems that Simon was just an average guy—a father of two who was likely visiting Jerusalem for the Passover, until a cross was placed on his back. This was not just any cross. This was the cross of Christ.

The cross that Simon carried was the greatest instrument of grace the world would ever know. It was the tool God would use to ransom the lost, held hostage by sin and death. This was the scene of the most important rescue mission there would ever be. This was the place where Jesus would die for Simon's sins and for the sins of his sons. The cross Simon carried was the place Jesus would pay the price for all your waywardness and for mine.

Jesus carried that cross for us. For the briefest of moments, Simon carried it for Him.

Before His disciples would watch in horror as their Savior was stapled to a wooden beam, He called all of His followers to follow His example of self-denial.

> "If anyone wants to follow after me . . ."

Every area of our life begs the same question, Do you want to follow Jesus? If the answer is yes . . .

> "Let him deny himself, take up his cross, and follow me." (Matt. 16:24)

The Christian life is and always will be a life of self-sacrifice. In denying ourselves, we declare there is One more worthy than our comfort, our desires, our selves. Fasting is like a free-weights exercise that builds our muscles of self-denial. We resist our natural craving for food; we temporarily reject the pull of full bellies; we lay down self and pick up suffering. Every time we do some reps, we see again that self-denial in the name of Jesus always comes with blessings. It shapes us more closely into His image. It reminds us of the sorrow Jesus chose for our sake.

Fasting is one small way we live like Jesus and carry a version of the burden He carried for us.

Simon, it seems, didn't have much choice. Christ's cross was shoved onto his back by force. You and I get to choose the path of self-denial as an expression of our obedience and love.

I ask again, Do you want to follow Jesus? If the answer is yes . . .

Deny yourself. Not just when it comes to food but when it comes to all sorts of things. Take up His cross and follow Him.

SETTING THE TABLE, INVITING THE FEAST

*Use the prayer prompts below to ask the Lord
to do an abundant work in your life.*

Setting the Table

*Jesus, thank You for picking up Your cross and carrying it to Calvary
for my sake. When I think of Your self-denial, I am amazed that
you . . .*

_____

_____

_____

_____

Inviting the Feast

*Lord, teach me how to deny myself and follow You. Whether in the
area of food or otherwise, show me what it means to pick up my
cross and follow You today. Even now, reveal where I am resisting
the call to sacrifice, and help me lay it down.*

Write down whatever comes to mind.

_____

_____

_____

_____

_____

_____

DAY 20

FEASTING

PLEASE PASS THE SELF-LOATHING

For no one ever hates his own flesh but provides and cares for it, just as Christ does for the church.

—Ephesians 5:29

My mom's Crock-Pot corn. (Yum!)

My Aunt Rhonda's pumpkin pie cake. (Double yum!)

My granny's cranberry salad. (Thanks, but no thanks.)

Each dish makes an annual appearance at my family's Thanksgiving dinner. There's a less appetizing tradition we also keep on repeat: a generational pattern of self-loathing. As the men move into the living room to catch the football game, the women fall into familiar conversations. We bemoan the food we just ate. We vow to diet in earnest in the new year. We joke that we removed the calories from the pumpkin pie. Though we smile and pat each other on the arm, inside no one is laughing.

Listen to the words one woman wrote to me. Do you see yourself in her story?

> I have struggled with food and body issues my whole life. I don't remember a time when I didn't feel ashamed of how I looked and even how I ate. I have studied Scriptures, read the good books, preached to myself, prayed, asked others to pray, started this plan and that diet plan and paid money I didn't have for this new guarantee of success....
>
> And yet, here I am. Starting over a new year with the same heart resolutions, praying and hoping that this will be the year the chains fall off.

Eat, regret, shame, repeat.

How many of us live in this perpetual spin cycle? Must we always live and eat this way? Hold that thought. Let's take a quick detour into the seemingly random subject of marriage.

READ EPHESIANS 5:22–33.

In these verses Paul gave practical instructions for how husbands and wives should interact:

> Wives, submit to your husbands as to the Lord. (v. 22)

> Husbands, love your wives, just as Christ loved the church and gave himself for her. (v. 25)

I don't believe Paul's goal was to provide a mini marriage counseling session. This passage is about something bigger and more eternal than wedded bliss. It shines a spotlight on a "profound mystery" (v. 32), the mystery of Christ's deep and lasting commitment to us.

The leap from marriage to food shame isn't as long as you might think. Look again at verse 29.

> For no one ever hates his own flesh but provides and
> cares for it, just as Christ does for the church.

Marriage is one diorama that tells the story of Christ's love. The way we treat our bodies is another. How we care for ourselves and nurture our bodies is meant to tell a story—the story of Christ's love. Once again the Bible offers a paradigm shift. Food and nutrition become messengers that remind us of the gospel and a means by which we can showcase Christ's love to others.

How does this speak into our shame? Pull out the photo album of God's Word and look at the pictures God has given us once again.

First, consider marriage. Is God most glorified by perfect marriages? I hope not, since no such thing exists. Our marriages put the gospel on display because despite our failures, despite our patterns of sin, despite the fact that we do not love each other perfectly, we keep our covenant commitment to each other, just as Jesus keeps His promise to stick with us in our sin. Imperfect marriages are like billboards that say, "We are bound together by love."

Is God most glorified by perfect bodies? Is the goal to eat perfectly (whatever that means)? No, God is glorified in our weaknesses. Imperfect food choices are like billboards that say, "[Christ's] grace is sufficient for you, for [His] power is perfected in weakness" (2 Cor. 12:9).

Food insecurity may be a lasting result of the fall. I still haven't outrun it. (I don't know any woman who has.) But shame doesn't have to pull up a seat to every table. We need not chase every meal with a serving of regret. More often than not, we do not fail on purpose with food; we don't run headlong toward failure. We stumble and trip, stumble and trip. Here is grace: when we stumble, we are caught up in Jesus' forever covenant with us, and we cannot break free from His love and commitment to help us through another day. The internal shift God's Word offers is this—our imperfect care of our bodies is a daily reminder of just how much we need the perfect love and grace of God.

SETTING THE TABLE, INVITING THE FEAST

*Use the prayer prompts below to ask the Lord
to do an abundant work in your life.*

Setting the Table

*Jesus, when I think of Your love and care for me, what comes to
mind is . . .*

_____

_____

_____

_____

_____

_____

_____

_____

_____

_____

_____

_____

_____

_____

_____

_____

_____

_____

Inviting the Feast

Lord, so often I let my weakness shift my focus toward myself. I see a better way in Your Word. My weaknesses are an opportunity to remind myself and others that You are . . .

_____

_____

_____

_____

_____

_____

_____

_____

_____

_____

_____

_____

_____

_____

_____

_____

_____

_____

_____

_____

....

....

A DIFFERENT KIND
OF RUNNER'S HIGH

*Therefore, since we are surrounded by so great a cloud of witnesses,
let us also lay aside every weight, and sin which clings so closely,
and let us run with endurance the race that is set before us,
looking to Jesus, the founder and perfecter of our faith, who for
the joy that was set before him endured the cross, despising the
shame, and is seated at the right hand of the throne of God.*

—Hebrews 12:1–3 ESV

The slice of cake I ate for breakfast on my fortieth birthday was the best thing I'd ever tasted.

It was good—a dense carrot cake with rich buttercream frosting—but the reason it tasted so exceptional was because it was the first bite of food I'd eaten in forty-one days.

As that milestone birthday approached, I knew I wanted it to mark more than my years of life. Assuming I will live to an average age, forty is a midpoint. That sobering reality moved me to seek the Lord with new fervor about how He wants me to live moving forward. If faith and life are a race, I want to run stronger and faster in the days ahead, not limp across the finish line. So I started a forty-day fast forty days before my fortieth birthday.

If I'm honest, I was hoping for a pep talk. Perhaps God would use the fast for a recommissioning of sorts? Instead, the Lord in His mercy used those forty days to put a magnifying glass over my sin. Relational tensions I'd disregarded as "normal"—or if not normal, then maybe excusable—suddenly needed to be dealt with. Habits I had long justified needed to go. As I ate less and prayed more, my heart was softened to areas of sin I had become calloused to.

Several months later, our toddler, Ezra, got lost temporarily. After a ten-minute search that felt like ten hours, we spotted him pushing his tricycle in a field near our home. Without a nanosecond of hesitation, I sprinted toward him, kicking off my sandals as I ran. I had a cardigan on; I tossed it aside. I flung my jewelry into the grass. I needed to run as fast as possible toward my boy—unhindered.

Later, as I sat with my Bible open, my eyes filled with grateful tears for God's protection. That forty-day fast came to mind. Hebrews 12:1–3 bubbled up in my heart.

> Let us also lay aside every weight, and sin which clings so closely, and let us run with endurance the race that is set before us, looking to Jesus, the founder and perfecter of our faith. (Heb. 12:1–2 ESV)

Suddenly the dots connected. I had, in fact, been recommissioned. God had dealt with my sin and my unhelpful habits so that I could run toward Him. Those forty days of fasting, though uncomfortable, kept me from running the remaining laps of my race slowed down by sins and patterns the Lord wanted to liberate me from.

READ ACTS 13:1–3.

Did you speed through those verses? We all face that temptation when we come to a list of names that not only represent people we've never met but are hard to pronounce! (I'm looking at you, Manaen.) But look again. What two activities are listed twice, once in verse 2 and once in verse 3?

These forefathers of the church were fasting and praying together. We don't know all of the reasons, but we can see one reason in the text—to set apart leaders for Christian service. Before Barnabas and Paul were unleashed by the Spirit to spread the gospel, they fasted and prayed with a small band of brothers.

Fasting is mysterious. We can't distill all the ways God can use it down into a simple, bulleted list, but we can know this for sure: *feasting on Jesus reduces our hunger for lesser things*. It fuels our passion to live our lives fully surrendered to His plan and for His glory.

Do you want to run unencumbered today? Can you picture your life like that moment when I ran singularly focused on getting to my little boy? Like a runner training for a marathon, we must develop regular rhythms that help us starve all that holds us back from running toward Christ, our prize. When we do, we will always discover the truth that He is the better portion—even better than carrot cake for breakfast.

SETTING THE TABLE, INVITING THE FEAST

*Use the prayer prompts below to ask the Lord
to do an abundant work in your life.*

Setting the Table

*Jesus, I want to crave You more and more and crave other things
less and less. Show me how.*

_____

_____

_____

_____

_____

_____

_____

_____

_____

_____

_____

_____

_____

_____

_____

_____

_____

Inviting the Feast

Lord, I am a sinner. Help me throw off anything in my life that makes me less effective in the race of faith. Will You show me, even now, what those hindrances are?

In the space below, list what He brings to mind by His Spirit or through His Word.

_____

_____

_____

_____

_____

_____

_____

_____

_____

_____

_____

_____

_____

_____

_____

_____

_____

_____

FEASTING

DIPPIN' DOTS FROM HEAVEN

*It resembled coriander seed, was white, and
tasted like wafers made with honey.*

—Exodus 16:31

For our oldest son's tenth birthday, we booked a train ride to the city of Chicago. It was a grand adventure for our little farm boy. We were eager to hold his hand as he discovered city museums, experienced his first taxi ride, and most importantly, enjoyed the new bliss of deep-dish pizza.

As we walked from our downtown hotel to our favorite Chicago pizza spot, I described the culinary experience he was about to have in vivid detail. "This is going to be epic!" I promised. He pulled a cheesy slice from the pie, and I sat on the edge of my seat, expecting his eyes to roll back in his head from the flavor. Imagine my surprise when he nonchalantly said instead, "I think I like Domino's pizza better."

READ EXODUS 16.

The Israelites had some food hang-ups. (Don't we all?) As soon as their hunger pangs hit, they suddenly forgot that they'd lived in Egypt as slaves, and they whined: "If only we had died by the LORD's hand in the land of Egypt, when we sat by pots of meat and ate all the bread we wanted. Instead, you brought us into this wilderness to make this whole assembly die of hunger!" (v. 3).

Despite their sniveling and regardless of their ingratitude, God provided. (Doesn't He always?) In His goodness God didn't simply replace their "pots of meat" and all-you-can-eat bread (which I doubt was an accurate memory of their diet as slaves). He gave them something altogether different, a miracle food no one had eaten before and no one has eaten since—manna.

Revisit verse 31. Jot down the description for manna.

_____

_____

_____

Excuse me while I go all gardening geek on you for a second. Coriander is the fruit of the Coriandrum sativum plant.[6] If you've ever whipped up a batch of guacamole, you've probably been closer to these seeds than you think: Cilantro is the leaf of the same plant. Coriander seeds look like little BBs.

Armed with that knowledge, picture the Israelites' reality. Every morning they woke up and found the ground covered in little white BBs. They were sweet and tasted like honey, like Dippin' Dots from heaven.

Did God expect the Israelites to receive this miracle with enthusiasm? Did He anticipate that they would sing with gratitude as they filled their bellies each morning with His unique and yummy gift? No, He knew the hearts of His children would not bend toward worship so easily. He still gave the gift. He still extended the invitation to feast.

It didn't take long for the Israelites to tire of their sweet miracle food. Numbers 11 records them grumbling again. This time they weren't just hungry. They were hungry for something *else*.

> "We remember the free fish we ate in Egypt, along with the cucumbers, melons, leeks, onions, and garlic. But now our appetite is gone; there's nothing to look at but this manna!" (vv. 5–6)

As broken people, we can't always discern the difference between fasting and feasting. Blessings and burdens get all mixed up together in God's providence for our lives. The Israelites convinced themselves that meat in slavery was a grander feast than manna in freedom just like my boy assumed a slice of plain ol' Domino's pizza was better than Chicago deep-dish.

The Israelites didn't have a food problem. They had a heart problem. Their ingratitude caused them to look at their food with a side helping of entitlement. They thought their issue was the quality of the outside elements they would put into their bodies, when really their issue was the quality of what was already inside of them.

Don't we repeat their patterns when we:

- Romanticize the idea that changing our diet will change our hearts?
- Grumble that we have to cook again or resent opportunities to feed others?
- Lose the wonder of God's provision for our physical and spiritual needs?
- Hunger more for a transformed outside than for a transformed inside?

Feasting doesn't just mean we eat lots of food. It goes beyond simply eating the foods we like best. No matter what we feast on, the truth is, it's all manna. It's all provided by God. Do you receive it with gratitude as evidence of His extravagant grace?

SETTING THE TABLE, INVITING THE FEAST

Use the prayer prompts below to ask the Lord
to do an abundant work in your life.

Setting the Table

*Jesus, I confess that I am prone to grumble about food. I can make
everything about the outside element of food instead of the interior
state of my heart. As I reflect on the complaints of the Israelites, I
see my own tendency to complain about . . .*

Inviting the Feast

Lord, You are a rich provider of manna to me, even today. The greatest food miracle You've worked in my own life is . . .

_____

_____

_____

_____

_____

_____

_____

_____

_____

_____

_____

_____

_____

_____

_____

_____

_____

_____

_____

_____

_____

_____

BREAK EVERY CHAIN

Isn't this the fast I choose:
To break the chains of wickedness,
to untie the ropes of the yoke,
to set the oppressed free,
and to tear off every yoke?

—Isaiah 58:6

It is a moment deeply seared into my spiritual memory. It was a hot summer night at church camp and the Bible teacher spoke on breaking chains.

- Chains of addiction
- Chains of bitterness
- Chains of depression
- Chains of anxiety
- Chains of fear
- Chains of sin . . .

Our hearts were stirred. By the power of the Holy Spirit, invisible links wrapped around our lives were exposed, and we became newly aware of our need for a Liberator.

We opened our Bibles and saw God's power to break every chain as rolls of crepe paper were passed among us. The teacher's instructions seemed silly at first; he asked us to wrap the crepe paper around our wrists as a symbol of whatever was holding us captive. Then, all at once, he gave the cue and we broke those bonds as an expression of our faith in God's power to set us free. Tears rolled down my cheeks and dampened the crepe paper on the floor. Truly God is a chain breaker, willing and able to unshackle us from every stronghold.

READ PSALM 107:10-16.

King David penned these words. He knew a thing or two about strongholds. Scripture tells us many stories of his fear and sin. His bonds were not made of crepe paper. He had been liberated from much more serious shackles. His heart was filled with praise for the God who set Him free. Could it be a coincidence that He also knew a thing or two about fasting (2 Sam. 12:16)?

Let's leave the Psalms and revisit Isaiah 58. You may remember that this passage is like a primer for true fasting, outlining the elements of fasting God will and won't accept. Look again at verse 6.

> Isn't this the fast I choose:
> To break the chains of wickedness,
> to untie the ropes of the yoke,
> to set the oppressed free,
> and to tear off every yoke?

God ultimately breaks every chain, but fasting is one way we participate in the process. It works like that church camp Bible teacher by reminding our spirit that Jesus can set us free. Fasting is an outward expression of our inward desire not to live shackled any more.

Are there strongholds in your life? There are some in mine.

- Strongholds of sin that need to be snapped
- Strongholds of bitterness, grief, and anger that need to be severed
- Strongholds of addiction that need to be smashed
- Strongholds of pride that need to be shattered . . .

Picture a hot auditorium filled with the people reading these words. Feel the weight of the chains wrapped around our lives. It doesn't have to be this way. There is a Liberator. The fast He has chosen for us breaks the chains of wickedness, sets the oppressed free, and tears off every yoke. When we fast, we participate with God in our liberation then stand back in awe as the chains hit the floor.

SETTING THE TABLE, INVITING THE FEAST

*Use the prayer prompts below to ask the Lord
to do an abundant work in your life.*

Setting the Table

*Holy Spirit, reveal any strongholds in my life. Write down whatever
comes to mind.*

_____

_____

_____

_____

Inviting the Feast

*Lord, I want to participate with You in my liberation. I want to fast
and pray not only for my own freedom from strongholds but for the
liberation of others, too. What would You have me fast from? For
how long? Lead me in the specifics, I pray.*

_____

_____

_____

_____

_____

_____

_____

_____

FEASTING

POP'S PRAYER

When you eat and are full, you will bless the Lord
your God for the good land he has given you.

—Deuteronomy 8:10

Our most kind and gracious Heavenly Father, we are indeed
grateful for Your many blessings. Please be with the loved
ones who are apart from us at this time, as we take this food
to the good of our bodies. In Jesus' name we pray. Amen.

My maternal grandfather, Roland (affectionately known as Pop) prayed these exact words before every meal. Whenever our family gathered in Granny and Pop's dining room, we'd hold hands in a big circle. Granny always started a version of the wave where each person squeezed the hand on their left as soon as they felt a squeeze from the right. Round and round the circle the affectionate squeezes would go as Pop slowly and intentionally repeated the familiar words. "Amen" was the signal to pick up our forks and dig in.

As I gather with my own children to eat, we pray a prayer my mom taught me as a child: "God is great. God is good. Let us thank Him for our food. Amen." If I open my eyes to peek, I always find one son trying to sneak a bite of food to his mouth before the prayer is over. I don't mind. It's a sweet tradition I hope my children repeat at their own dining room tables someday.

READ DEUTERONOMY 8:1–20.

The first five books of the Bible, called the Torah, were penned by Moses. Deuteronomy is the last of those five books. Originally written to the Israelites and mercifully preserved for us, Deuteronomy contains God's instructions for how to thrive in the land of promise. Once again food is a prominent theme.

> For the LORD your God is bringing you into a good land, a land with streams, springs, and deep water sources, flowing in both valleys and hills; a land of wheat, barley, vines, figs, and pomegranates; a land of olive oil and honey; a land where you will eat food without shortage, where you will lack nothing. (vv. 7–9)

Note the order of God's instructions for food and prayer.

> When you eat and are full, you will bless the LORD your God for the good land he has given you. (v. 10)

Maybe my sons have it right. The invitation in this text is to eat first and pray second, to bless God for the food once we've tasted it on our tongues. This is not a mandate, requiring us to stop praying before our meals. There's no sense getting legalistic since God's Word tells us to "pray constantly" (1 Thess. 5:17). But these verses are yet another reminder that food is a gift meant to turn our hearts in gratitude toward God.

I once met a man who told me he prayed as he carried in his groceries. He figured that way he was covered if he ever forgot to pray during a meal. I laughed at the time, but now I see his habit as a helpful one. Pray when you're hungry. Pray when you're full. Pray when you're buying groceries, and pray when you're carrying them in. Pray as you cook your supper, and pray as you clear the table after the meal.

A holistic view of Scripture leads toward a more holistic view of food. We pray when we need food as an expression of our trust in God to provide. We pray when we receive food as an expression of our awe that God has met our needs again. We pray after we eat food as an expression of our gratitude for God's good gifts. Pray and eat. Eat and pray. This is a rhythm God has built into our lives.

What rhythms exist in your own life for food and prayer? What new rhythms can you begin?

SETTING THE TABLE, INVITING THE FEAST

*Use the prayer prompts below to ask the Lord
to do an abundant work in your life.*

_____

Setting the Table

*Jesus, as I consider my rhythms of food and prayer, I now realize
that . . .*

_____

_____

_____

_____

_____

Inviting the Feast

*Using a combination of what you know about God from His Word
and what He is stirring in your heart, write out your own version of
Pop's Prayer. (Pop won't mind.)*

_____

_____

_____

_____

_____

_____

_____

....

FASTING

....

GODWARD NOT INWARD

*"Therefore I tell you: Don't worry about your life, what you will eat
or what you will drink; or about your body, what you will wear.
Isn't life more than food and the body more than clothing?"*

—Matthew 6:25

It started as counting calories and picking up an extra exercise class or two. I was a college sophomore who wanted to lose a few pounds. Those desires seemed benign enough, but it didn't take them long to evolve into something much more destructive. Before I knew it, I had developed a full-blown eating disorder.

While plenty of people noticed the changes to my body, only a few saw the changes in my heart. I became food obsessed, but that was just the first, most visible layer of the onion. You had to peel that back to get to the real issue—I had become obsessed with myself. Thinking about food and exercise all the time were the gateway drugs my pride-filled heart needed to get high on an infatuation with me.

Let's revisit Jesus' Sermon on the Mount. (Who knew there was so much there about our relationship with food?)

READ MATTHEW 6:25–34.

Face it: we've got a lot of food worries. We worry we're eating the wrong foods. We worry we're not eating the right foods. We worry about our grocery bills. We worry about our kids' nutrition. We worry food will make us gain weight. We worry food will make us sick. . . . Food and worry. Worry and food.

Jesus hit this cycle head on.

> "So don't worry, saying, 'What will we eat?' or 'What will we drink?' or 'What will we wear?' For the Gentiles eagerly seek all these things, and your heavenly Father knows that you need them." (vv. 31–32)

Jesus was preaching in Israel to listeners who viewed Gentiles as those who lived outside the favor of God. In saying, "The Gentiles eagerly seek these things," Jesus was saying that food worry is the activity of the faithless. In contrast, laying aside our worry about food is evidence of our trust in the Lord. I understand the theory but struggle to live it out in real time. Jesus showed us how.

> "But seek first the kingdom of God and his righteousness, and all these things will be provided for you." (v. 33)

It's paradoxical but true: I was far more worried about food as an anorexic college girl than I am as a slightly chubby forty-something. The reasons go beyond maturity. (I know plenty of food-obsessed women in my age bracket.) The real shift happened in my focus, not my fat cells.

Food worries are often the mask we wear to cover our self-obsession. Because of the ways pride warps our thinking, it's so easy to focus on us. Jesus offers a better way.

Fasting turns our hearts Godward. Dieting can only ever turn our hearts inward.

It's not ultimately about the food. Do you want to be free of food worries? Seek first the kingdom of God, not the kingdom of self. When we turn Godward, not inward, we're making a statement of faith that God alone is worthy of our obsession.

SETTING THE TABLE, INVITING THE FEAST

*Use the prayer prompts below to ask the Lord
to do an abundant work in your life.*

Setting the Table

*Jesus, when I consider my own relationship with food, I see evidence
of my obsession with myself in these ways . . .*

_____

_____

_____

_____

Inviting the Feast

*Lord, I want to seek Your kingdom instead of mine. Would You
meet me right now and give me some next steps toward this? What
practical things might help me turn my attention toward You and
Your kingdom?*

Write down whatever comes to mind.

_____

_____

_____

_____

_____

_____

_____

FEASTING

THE GIRLS AT
YOUR TABLE

*One generation will declare your works to the next
and will proclaim your mighty acts.*

—Psalm 145:4

My grandmother ate a tapeworm *on purpose.*

Food worries have wreaked havoc on the women of my family for generations. Growing up, I thought dieting was the norm. I watched the women in my family go on every diet imaginable. I heard their constant negative comments about their weight.

It's part of our family lore that before the FDA regulated such things, my grandmother took diet pills that were actually tapeworms. She lost weight (as hosts for parasitic invaders tend to), but I wonder what it cost her heart (and body) to go to such great lengths to tame The Food Beast. She passed her distorted views to her daughters, including my mother, in a painful version of trickle-down emotional economics.

READ PSALM 145.

When we get offtrack about the source of our value, it's not ulti-mately about the numbers on the scale or the food on our plates. Maybe it's not your weight that makes you question your worth. Perhaps you gauge your value by:

- The size of your house
- Your ability to "manage" your to-do list
- What others think of you
- Your current sense of self-confidence
- How many plates you can keep spinning
- How your kids are doing in their academic or social development
- How high on the ladder you have climbed at work

These are all pain points of the same problem—we don't believe God's Word.

- Psalm 139:14 says that you were made with fear and wonder.
- First Corinthians 6:20 says that you were bought with a price.
- Matthew 10:29–32 says God values you highly.
- Ephesians 2:10 says you were created by the Master Artisan.

When it comes to biblical evidence of your value to God, these verses are just the tip of the iceberg. Notice: they have nothing to do with food. They have nothing to do with weight.

Here's a heavy question: Could a woman rooted in the belief that her value comes from God ingest a tapeworm to shed some pounds? Here's a difficult answer: no. When we use food as a means to exert control over our life, when we operate out of shame about our body, when we see food as a cross to carry instead of a means of God-infused grace—we're revealing that there are areas of our life where our roots are shallow, too. When we fail to operate out of our worth in Christ, there is always collateral damage. Insecurity is contagious. The girls in your life are especially susceptible to catching yours.

Who are the girls gathered around your proverbial table? Are they your daughters? Your granddaughters? Your nieces? Your neighbors? Your friends? Make no mistake, their eyes are on you.

As women of faith, we have a responsibility to carry the banner for the next generation. God has commanded us to hold high our stories of His goodness. The runoff from our lives meant to trickle into their hearts is not food and diet obsession. It's not worth based on weight.

This one's for the girls. May they see us holding high the banner of this remarkable truth:

> So God created man
> in his own image;
> he created him in the image of God;
> he created them male and female. (Gen. 1:27)

SETTING THE TABLE, INVITING THE FEAST

*Use the prayer prompts below to ask the Lord
to do an abundant work in your life.*

Setting the Table

Lord, if I could sum up the legacy of food in my own family, I'd put it this way . . .

_____

_____

_____

_____

_____

_____

_____

_____

_____

_____

_____

_____

_____

_____

_____

_____

Inviting the Feast

Jesus, I pray You'll bring faces to mind of other women who could learn about Your love as they watch my life, particularly my relationship with food (and the way I talk about it). When I think of them, I realize just how much I want to hold high the banner of Your truth to the next generation. Give me direction, even now, on how I might do this.

Write about or draw a picture of what that could look like.

_____

_____

_____

_____

_____

_____

_____

_____

_____

_____

_____

_____

_____

_____

_____

_____

_____

_____

....

FASTING

....

I WILL NOT BE
MASTERED

"Everything is permissible for me," but not everything is beneficial.
"Everything is permissible for me," but I will not be mastered by anything.

—1 Corinthians 6:12

I t's cold in my office this morning. As I write these words, I'm wearing wool socks and sipping the perfect cup of tea. It's Earl Grey, steeped just long enough and with a touch of honey, steamed milk, and a dash of cinnamon—one of God's first gifts of the day.

READ 1 CORINTHIANS 6:12–13.

As we open our Bible once again to consider faith and food, Paul's words are a reminder that in the tea of life, the gospel is not the honey. It's not a little something sweet we might add when we're in the mood. It's not the dollop of whipped cream on top or a dash of something extra. The gospel is the tea leaves, *infused* into everything we believe, think, and do. Scripture calls us to operate steeped and saturated with the good news of Christ's work in our lives.

Bible scholars think Corinthian believers were fond of a certain saying—one that went something like: "Everything is permissible for me." Through the teaching of Paul and the apostles, these new Christians had only recently discovered the doctrine of grace. How liberating that must have felt! So much so that they faced the temptation to use grace as a permission slip for sin. Paul's words lend an essential balance.

Yes, it's true that Jesus made a way for us to be redeemed by grace through faith (Eph. 2:8–9). This really is good news because as sinners we are incapable of earning righteousness by perfectly keeping God's perfect law. But when we see grace as a blank check to do whatever we want, we miss the reason God gave us the law in the first place. Every command is for our good. Following the law of God results in our thriving.

This truth reminds me of parenting. My children would eat cotton candy for breakfast every morning if they could. That wouldn't make me any less their mother. I'd still love them with my whole heart. I'd still care for their needs. I'd still be fiercely devoted to them, but they'd have bellyaches. Their growth would stunt. Their teeth would rot and fall out.

This is a picture for what Paul is describing in these verses. Good things become bad things when they control us. Money is God's provision, but when it masters us, we become its slave. Work is God's gift, but when it masters us, it becomes a heavy burden. Relationships are God's gift, but when they master us, we let them be the boss of us. This is why every part of our lives needs a gospel infusion.

We have the opportunity to practice the mastery of loving God's law and living under the doctrine of grace every day with food. Sure, a caffeine addiction is permissible for you. You can drink twenty cups a day, and God won't love you any less. But it isn't beneficial. Yep, you can eat ten thousand calories a day if you want to. God will still meet your needs, but your God-given body won't. You will struggle to live the abundant life Christ offers. Sure, eat cotton candy for breakfast, but you're gonna have a bellyache.

We often approach food with our own version of the Corinthians mantra ever wondering, "Can't I just eat what I want?" The answer is, "Yes you can" *but while the Bible gives us answers, it also gives us better questions:*

- When it comes to food, what masters you?
- When it comes to food, what is *best* for you?

Jesus invites us into a rhythm of self-denial not motivated by fear of violating the law but motivated by gratitude for the extravagant grace we've been given. Only when our lives are infused with the gospel are we able to face food's many temptations with balance.

Fasting is one way we can show food who the boss is. For a meal or a day or week, when we fast, we stand up to food and say, "I will not be mastered." It is not a ritual. It is not a rule. It is a choice to operate from what is beneficial instead of simply what is permissible. For the follower of Christ, embracing the practice of fasting is one way we can live a life perfectly steeped in gospel truth.

SETTING THE TABLE, INVITING THE FEAST

*Use the prayer prompts below to ask the Lord
to do an abundant work in your life.*

Setting the Table

Lord, show me areas where I've been mastered by food.

Write down whatever comes to mind.

_____

_____

_____

_____

_____

_____

_____

_____

_____

_____

_____

_____

_____

_____

_____

_____

_____

Inviting the Feast

Jesus, show me where I've been operating according to what is permissible instead of what is beneficial, and teach me how to do the opposite. I cannot do this without Your help.

_____

_____

_____

_____

_____

_____

_____

_____

_____

_____

_____

_____

_____

_____

_____

_____

_____

_____

_____

_____

_____

_____

_____

FEASTING

ODD BEDFELLOWS

*Don't you know that your body is a temple of the Holy Spirit who
is in you, whom you have from God? You are not your own.*

—1 Corinthians 6:19

Let's keep our hearts in park and stay in 1 Corinthians 6 for another
day. There is more wisdom to be gleaned from this passage.

READ 1 CORINTHIANS 6:12–20.

What do you see as the two primary themes of this passage? Record
your response.

_____

_____

Survey says? Food and sex. What odd bedfellows. But are they?

Paul's firm reminder, "Don't you know that your body is a temple of
the Holy Spirit who is in you, whom you have from God?" is quoted
often for good reason. He is warning us to steer clear of sexual sin

because of the ways it violates God's best for our bodies. Pay attention to how this verse is used among modern Christians, and you'll often hear the wires cross. Healthy eaters espouse, "My body is a temple," as their motivation for eating greens and shunning sugar. Not-so-healthy eaters sarcastically joke, "My body is a temple," as a way of sheepishly acknowledging, "I shouldn't be eating this." But Paul's temple reference wasn't about food, right? The more I look at the passage, the more I realize the answer is yes—and no.

If we extract single verses from the bigger narrative of Scripture, we might miss that Paul wrote these words as one train of thought. He starts with food, a more daily and seemingly insignificant area of our lives where our beliefs and behaviors can go sideways:

> "Food is for the stomach and the stomach for food,"
> and God will do away with both of them. (v. 13)

Notice he mentions food right before he takes a hard right to sexual sin and sleeping with prostitutes.

> Don't you know that your bodies are part of Christ's body? So should I take a part of Christ's body and make it part of a prostitute? Absolutely not! (v. 15)

How are these threads connected? Here's my theory: what we think about food tends to reveal what we think about everything else. Said another way, if we think the body is permitted to have anything and everything it craves when it comes to food, we'll tend to apply that thinking to all sorts of other things. Look at the whole passage once more. Use food as a grid to consider these themes:

- There is a better question than what is "allowed." That question is, What is best?
- A follower of Christ who is mastered by something, who is mastered by anything, needs Spirit-fueled self-control.

- Our bodies, as we know them right now in their fallen state, are temporary. We're called to live for what's eternal.
- We belong to Jesus: body, soul, and spirit.

If we are not living out these truths in our daily approach to food, we likely aren't living them out elsewhere. Wrong thinking about God and food is often also wrong thinking about God and sex, God and rest, God and exercise. . . . You get the idea. "Your body is a temple" is not an invitation to shape yourself into the perfect physical specimen. It is a reminder that Christ lives in you. That supernatural, metaphysical reality should be evident in the way we live our natural, physical lives.

What we eat and who we sleep with, what we say and what we watch, where we go and what we drink when we get there—these are all opportunities to declare one heart-shaping, world-changing, life-transforming truth:

> You are not your own, for you were bought at a price.
> So glorify God with your body. (vv. 19–20)

SETTING THE TABLE, INVITING THE FEAST

*Use the prayer prompts below to ask the Lord
to do an abundant work in your life.*

Setting the Table

*Jesus, I now see the ways my thinking about food reveals my
thinking about other things. Specifically . . .*

_____

_____

_____

_____

_____

_____

_____

_____

_____

_____

_____

_____

_____

_____

_____

_____

_____

Inviting the Feast

Lord, I don't always know what it means to "glorify God with your body" in the context of everyday life. Will You show me, please? Give me ideas for how to do this in the coming days and months.

Write down what comes to mind.

_____

_____

_____

_____

_____

_____

_____

_____

_____

_____

_____

_____

_____

_____

_____

_____

_____

_____

_____

....

FASTING

....

NO ARM TWISTING

His servants asked him, "Why have you done this? While the baby was alive, you fasted and wept, but when he died, you got up and ate food."

—2 Samuel 12:21

It was one of those moments where time seems suspended and everyone reacts in slow motion. I was on the ultrasound table with my pregnant belly covered in clear goo. My husband was by my side, and a doctor was standing in front of us with a clipboard, telling us our baby wasn't going to make it. Shock and fear and grief swirled together into desperate prayers.

Our baby survived. He is a thriving teenager now, but I can empathize with the emotions David must have felt when he heard the news that his child was going to die.

READ 2 SAMUEL 12.

When confronted with his sin and the sickness and sorrow it caused, David responded with prayer and fasting (v. 16). This passage gives us some additions to our growing list of biblical reasons to fast:

- We fast in repentance.
- We fast in grief.
- We fast when we are desperate for God to intervene.
- We fast when our sin hurts others.
- We fast when someone we love is deathly ill.
- We fast when shock and fear and grief swirl together into desperate prayers.

Scripture gives us every reason to believe that David's fast was a sign of true repentance. His desire for his sick child to live was surely a noble desire. And yet,

> On the seventh day the baby died. (v. 18)

From this story we learn that fasting is not a formula. We can't add fasting to our prayers and find God always answers them the way we want Him to. We can't subtract the consequences of our sin by adding fasting to repentance. While God can use fasting to change us, the reverse is never true—we cannot use fasting as a tool to change the character of God.

Like David, Job learned this lesson as he sat in the dust of circumstances, he was powerless to change. He declared, "I know you can do anything and no plan of yours can be thwarted" (Job 42:2).

God wants our prayers. God hears our prayers. God responds to our prayers. But God never relinquishes control. No amount of prayer and fasting can supersede His sovereignty. We cannot twist the arm of God.

So, did David fast in vain? No, because nothing done for the Lord is ever wasted.

> Then David got up from the ground. He washed, anointed himself, changed his clothes, went to the LORD's house, and worshiped. Then he went home

and requested something to eat. So they served him
food, and he ate. (2 Sam. 12:20)

Fasting and prayer may not have saved his baby boy, but perhaps they
saved David. God used those facedown moments of desperate hunger
to feed David's heart. The hours spent fasting and praying prepared
David to receive the news that his child was dead. He walked through
the door of grief and straight into the house of God with a heart bent
toward worship. It may not have been the miracle he was fasting for,
but it was certainly miraculous.

We don't embrace fasting as a means to get more of what we want
from God. We embrace fasting as a means to give Him more of what
He wants from us.

- More of our prayers
- More of our focus
- More of our sacrifice
- More of our faith
- More of our time
- More of our intimacy

No, we cannot twist God's arm. He's much too strong for that. But
He can mold and shape us more into His image when we obediently lay
our lives into His sovereign hands.

SETTING THE TABLE, INVITING THE FEAST

*Use the prayer prompts below to ask the Lord
to do an abundant work in your life.*

Setting the Table

*Jesus, as I reflect on David's response to sin and suffering, I am
moved by his example. What type of grief might You be calling me
to process via fasting?*

_____

_____

_____

_____

_____

_____

_____

_____

_____

_____

_____

_____

_____

_____

_____

_____

Inviting the Feast

Lord, I know You can do anything and no plan of yours can be thwarted. I praise You for Your sovereignty.

_____

_____

_____

_____

_____

_____

_____

_____

_____

_____

_____

_____

_____

_____

_____

_____

_____

_____

_____

_____

_____

_____

_____

FEASTING

CRUNCHY GRANOLA AND THE GOSPEL

Not that there is another gospel.

—Galatians 1:7

My husband and I are the proud owners of a little farm in the middle of the Midwest. We raise and butcher our own cows and chickens, eat eggs straight from the coop every morning, and grow our own green beans. Each year we add a few trees to our fruit orchard so more peach juice can dribble down our chins all summer and more pesticide-free apples can fill our fruit bowl all fall. I make jam from our organic blackberries and elderberry syrup from the berry patch in our backyard. I know the image you are picturing, and I probably look just like her. Yes, my favorite shoes are Birkenstocks. Yes, my hair is usually in a braid. Yes, I care about food. But I care more about the church, and I fear we're dying on all the wrong hills.

When I am with my Christian sisters, the conversation turns toward food more often than not. Someone is trying keto. Someone else is cutting caffeine. This friend is trying intermittent fasting to lose weight.

That one is sick and tired of feeling sick and tired. While I acknowledge that healthy eating is an important part of healthy living (I'm a crunchy granola farmer, remember?), I also think we need to recalibrate. In a world where everything seems like a big hairy deal, we are wise to remember that there are mountains and there are molehills. Pile all of the gluten in the world and stack it up next to the message the world needs most, and it's still just a molehill.

READ GALATIANS 1:6–10.

The Galatians were apparently operating from a warped version of the gospel. Any time we believe salvation comes from Jesus and (fill in the blank), we repeat their mistake.

- The gospel and good works cannot save us.
- The gospel and political solutions cannot save us.
- The gospel and our self-esteem cannot save us.
- The gospel and living our dreams cannot save us.

And, in the ultimate sense, the gospel and our food choices cannot save us.

Several years ago I made some significant food changes with significant physical results. My energy skyrocketed. My skin cleared up. My pants got looser. An inner monologue began: "This is amazing! It's going to change everything. My relationships are going to be better. I'm going to be able to work longer hours. Pretty soon I will look like a supermodel." I started talking about food more incessantly and with greater passion than almost anything else. I didn't say it exactly this way, but I had shifted my hope, believing that changes in my diet could fix what only God can.

Galatians gives us a vital gut check: "Not that there is another gospel." Christ alone saves us from our brokenness. Food matters, but it does not matter supremely.

Gluten is not God, nor is it the Antichrist. Cutting grain or sugar might make us feel better, and it can surely be healthier for us in certain seasons, but it is not a long-term path to wholeness. We can't experience true restoration by eating cage-free eggs.

Yes, I grow my own food. Yes, I live a lifestyle of farm to table, but that's not what I want on my tombstone. I want to live for and point others toward the one and only gospel—the gospel of Jesus Christ. Join me.

SETTING THE TABLE, INVITING THE FEAST

*Use the prayer prompts below to ask the Lord
to do an abundant work in your life.*

Setting the Table

*Jesus, just like the Galatians, my heart turns away from You so
easily. I realize I've been looking for true restoration in these
things . . .*

_____

_____

_____

_____

_____

Inviting the Feast

*Lord, teach me to rightly prioritize food and everything else in my
life. You are the only source of ultimate hope.*

_____

_____

_____

_____

_____

_____

_____

THE SAFEST PLACE

Yet when they were sick, my clothing was sackcloth;
I humbled myself with fasting, and my prayer was genuine.

—Psalm 35:13

READ PSALM 35.

David's enemies carried swords. They literally wanted to kill him (v. 4).

Try to stand in his position for a moment. How would you respond to that level of opposition? Would you:

- Return threat for threat?
- Rally allies?
- Grow embittered?
- Operate from fight-or-flight impulses?

David fasted.

This psalm recounts all the ways David had been wronged. He didn't shy away from asking the Lord to intervene:

> Let those who intend to take my life
> be disgraced and humiliated. (v. 4)

And,

> Let their way be dark and slippery,
> with the angel of the LORD pursuing them. (v. 6)

And,

> Let ruin come on him unexpectedly,
> and let the net that he hid ensnare him. (v. 8)

Yet when the same enemies he prayed to see fall faced hardship, David didn't flex. He prayed and fasted.

> Yet when they were sick,
> my clothing was sackcloth;
> I humbled myself with fasting,
> and my prayer was genuine.
> I went about mourning as if for my friend or brother;
> I was bowed down with grief,
> like one mourning for a mother. (vv. 13–14)

As I consider how this dichotomy speaks into our lives, a memory bubbles up in my heart. Several years ago I sat in a counselor's office mad as a hornet. A family member had wronged me. Her sins against me were serious, and I had legitimate reasons to be hurt and angry. With deep compassion, rooted in God's truth, the counselor looked at me and said, "Trust her to Jesus. It's the safest place for her to be."

Every defense mechanism fell to the floor. Every recourse I'd been imagining suddenly felt too small. I didn't have to pursue vigilante justice in person or in my heart. Her words were a jarring and comforting reminder that God has promised to deliver us from our enemies

(Ps. 34:7), surrendering our desires for them is the ultimate proof that our hope is in Him.

Throughout His Word, God commands us to respond to those who hurt us in ways that often feel counterintuitive:

- "Be quiet" (Exod. 14:14).
- "If your enemy is hungry, give him food to eat, and if he is thirsty, give him water to drink" (Prov. 25:21).
- "If anyone slaps you on your right cheek, turn the other to him also" (Matt. 5:39).
- "Love your enemies and pray for those who persecute you" (Matt. 5:44).
- "Bless those who persecute you; bless and do not curse" (Rom. 12:14).

Each one of these steps requires us to relinquish our illusion of control over others and to lay them, emotionally speaking, into the palms of God. Fasting for our enemies is not overtly commanded, but David shows us the beauty in it. He had legitimate reasons to be angry and afraid. His enemies wronged him relentlessly. His heartbeat is with the Lord's in both his prayers for God-orchestrated vindication and in his fasting for his enemy's sake.

Fasting is an act of surrender. We lay down what we can control, namely the food we put in our mouths, and place our hope in what God can control, namely everything else.

Your enemies may not carry swords. Their weapons might be sharp words or unfair criticism or catty gossip. Have you ever fasted for them? It is a step of humility—a challenging step of surrender for sure—but you can trust your enemies to Jesus. It's the safest place for them to be.

SETTING THE TABLE, INVITING THE FEAST

*Use the prayer prompts below to ask the Lord
to do an abundant work in your life.*

Setting the Table

*Lord, I know Your hands are the safest place for my enemies to be. I
entrust these enemies to You right now . . .*

Inviting the Feast

Lord, are there any "enemies" You want me to fast and pray for? What specific things might you want me to intercede for on their behalf?

Write down whatever comes to mind.

_____

_____

_____

_____

_____

_____

_____

_____

_____

_____

_____

_____

_____

_____

_____

_____

_____

_____

_____

FEASTING

WORTHY OF OUR BEST

"You are to bring the first sheaf of your harvest to the priest."
—Leviticus 23:10

Is there something seasonal you look forward to each year? Maybe that first bite of watermelon in the summer or the first sip of pumpkin spice latte in the fall? Now, picture bringing that first bite or that first sip to the Lord as an expression of your desire to give Him your best.

In Leviticus 23, as God was describing the seven feasts to Moses, He called His children into a specific act of worship—surrendering firstfruits.

READ LEVITICUS 23:9–14.

If the language of this feast feels too agrarian, force your brain to remember that for the Israelites, their crops were their food. There were no grocery stores or restaurant chains in the promised land. So while this was a feast about farming, it was ultimately a feast about food.

We can simplify the heartbeat of the Feast of Firstfruits this way: **Give God your best, for He is surely worthy.**

It is not accidental that the Bible uses food to teach us firstfruit patterns of worship.

> So, whether you eat or drink, or whatever you do, do
> everything for the glory of God. (1 Cor. 10:31)

As followers of Jesus, we are called to expand the Feast of Firstfruits beyond an annual ritual to every area of our lives, from the most mundane tasks to the biggest steps of obedience. We eat and drink for God's glory. We work and play for God's glory. We serve and sacrifice for God's glory. The mantle God has placed on our shoulders is for His glory to become paramount and for us to search for ways to point to Him all day, every day.

God didn't establish the Feast of Firstfruits because He needed flour and grain. He established the Feast of Firstfruits because *we* need to be reminded that our lives belong to Him and He is worthy of our best.

As you look at your life, are the Bible's words true of you? Whether you eat or drink, do you do it all for the glory of God? If you're feeling the need to make adjustments to give God your first fruits more fully, be encouraged. A beautiful second layer to the Feast of Firstfruits is this: God always gives second fruits. The Israelites gave God their first sheaf of grain. He gave them fields and fields of wheat. We seek to give God glory in the way we approach food. He satisfies us with the Bread of Life. We bring Him our best; He gives us Himself.

SETTING THE TABLE, INVITING THE FEAST

*Use the prayer prompts below to ask the Lord
to do an abundant work in your life.*

Setting the Table

*Jesus, I want to give You my best. I surrender anew the firstfruits of
every area of my life including . . .*

_____

_____

_____

_____

_____

_____

_____

_____

_____

_____

_____

_____

_____

_____

_____

_____

_____

Inviting the Feast

God, thank You for the abundance of Your blessings in my life. I am especially grateful for Your gifts of . . .

DAY 33

....

FASTING

....

THE SECRET FAST

Your Father who sees in secret will reward you.

—Matthew 6:18

When it comes to conversations about fasting, it seems we've developed a collective nervous tic. Despite the fact that fasting is mentioned more than a hundred times in Scripture, the topic often feels off-limits in our modern faith circles. I have a hunch that we can blame that on our understanding of Matthew 6.

READ MATTHEW 6:16–18.

Jesus gives two instructions for how His followers should fast: "Put oil on your head" and "Wash your face." If hygiene tips feel disconnected from your own questions about how to fast, take note: Jesus was advocating for scrubbed hearts more than clean faces.

As we've seen on other pages of our Bibles, not every fast is a God-honoring fast. Jesus called out hypocrites who used fasting as a means to get attention from others. They made themselves look terrible on purpose, publicly donning gloomy, dirty, sullen faces for all to see. They broadcasted the hardship of their fast in hopes that someone would notice, ask them what's wrong, and give the hypocrite a chance to toss out a humble brag, "Ohhhh, I'm juuust fasting." Translation: "Look how deeply spiritual I am." Because the Lord is always more concerned with our heart than our behavior, this kind of fasting doesn't please Him. He lovingly offers an alternative. We turn our hearts Godward, toward the right object of our adoration, not manward, seeking applause from others.

But what about all that "secret" business?

> So that your fasting isn't obvious to others but to your Father who is in secret. And your Father who sees in secret will reward you. (v. 18)

Read those words again. More carefully this time. What is Jesus really saying about the part of fasting that's secret? It is not the fast itself. It is the Father whose face is hidden from us (for now).

For far too long, I fear that our aversion to *talking about fasting* has led to an aversion to fasting itself. Certainly if you're going to fast, don't brag about it. And if you do brag, repent, believe the gospel, and try again. But let's put this subject back on the table, shall we?

Jesus never told us to pursue strictly secret fasts. How could He when so much of His Word calls God's people to fast together in observable ways (mourning together, wearing sackcloth and ashes, etc.)? What Jesus *did* encourage us to do, however, was to always seek strictly secret rewards. The kind that other people can never give. The kind that the Father who sees in secret gives so generously.

SETTING THE TABLE, INVITING THE FEAST

*Use the prayer prompts below to ask the Lord
to do an abundant work in your life.*

Setting the Table

*Jesus, I've been nervous about fasting because I've been afraid
people will think I . . .*

_____

_____

_____

_____

_____

_____

_____

_____

_____

_____

_____

_____

_____

_____

_____

_____

_____

_____

Inviting the Feast

Lord, help me approach fasting and every other area of my life more concerned about what You think than what others think. Help me seek the kinds of reward and approval and praise that come from You and not other people. I don't think I've been doing that in the areas of . . .

_____

_____

_____

_____

_____

_____

_____

_____

_____

_____

_____

_____

_____

_____

_____

_____

_____

_____

_____

FEASTING

THE LAST SUPPER

"This is my body, which is given for you.
Do this in remembrance of me."

—Luke 22:19

The last thing Jesus did with His friends before He was arrested was to gather and share a good meal.

READ LUKE 22:14–22.

Since we have the whole Bible at our fingertips, we know the rest of the story. After the disciples gathered in the Upper Room to observe the Passover meal together, all hell literally broke loose. But suspend time in your mind for a moment. Don't rush past the meaning of this moment.

Smell the unleavened bread Jesus broke and handed to His brethren. Picture holding the shared cup of wine in your hands and then passing it to a friend you love.

As He does so often in Scripture, Jesus used food to teach lessons of eternal significance. The disciples didn't yet have the full context for what Jesus was showing them when He said:

> "This is my body, which is given for you." (v. 19)

They couldn't grasp the gravity of His words when He commanded:

> "This cup is the new covenant in my blood, which is poured out for you." (v. 20)

We are blessed to be able to peer through the looking glass of the gospel and see that Jesus was using the common act of eating and drinking to reveal His plan to redeem the world. It wasn't truly the last supper, for we will feast with Jesus again soon (Rev. 19:6–9). It was the last supper without resurrection hope. The next time Jesus gathered with His friends for a meal (John 21:1–14), He had died for the sins of the world and triumphed over death. This was not the Last Supper; *this was the Lord's Supper.*

Two thousand years later, we observe Christ's command to "do this in remembrance of me" (v. 19) every time we take Communion. We take a tiny cracker and a little cup of juice as symbols of the sacrifice of our Savior. In my church this is a weekly observance. Yours might be quarterly or once a month, but as I read the Last Supper account, I wonder if Communion moments with our local congregation might form us into people who remember gospel truths not only at the Lord's Table but every table. What if we became people who, every time we eat, think of Jesus' body broken for us and the price He paid for our sin? What if, every time we drink, we remembered that He poured out His blood to rescue us? What if every time we gathered, we reminded one another that He would do anything to redeem us from death?

What if every bite of food and every sip of a drink could remind us that we are welcome at God's table because Jesus left the Upper Room and went to the cross for us? It is good to consider Jesus every time the Communion tray is passed, but Christ's triumph is worth celebrating well beyond Sunday morning.

Every time you set the table . . .

Every time you gather to eat a meal with friends . . .

Every time you eat . . .

Every time you drink . . .

You can operate in the spirit of the Lord's Supper.

> And he took bread, gave thanks, broke it, gave it to them, and said, "This is my body, which is given for you. Do this in remembrance of me." (v. 19)

SETTING THE TABLE, INVITING THE FEAST

*Use the prayer prompts below to ask the Lord
to do an abundant work in your life.*

Setting the Table

*Jesus, thank You for allowing Your body to be broken and Your
blood to be spilled for me. Today, I pause to remember Your
sacrifice.*

Inviting the Feast

*Lord, help the daily acts of eating and drinking to become more
meaningful to me. Show me how to remember the gospel each time
I make a meal, gather with others, or enjoy a dinner with friends.*

....

FASTING

....

STOMACH GOD

Their god is their stomach.

—Philippians 3:19

We live in a food-obsessed world. We photograph our meals. Chefs are celebrities. Cookbooks make the list of *New York Times* best sellers.

In a culture where "foodie" is worn like a badge of honor, we have an opportunity to point to the One who offers more than full stomachs—the One who offers full hope.

READ PHILIPPIANS 3:12–21.

This passage contrasts two kinds of people: those for whom this fallen earth feels like home and those of us who know that the world as we know it is not where we belong. As Christ's followers, we are always reaching heavenward, toward the permanent comforts of life in Him. In contrast, those who do not know Jesus reach toward temporary comforts that can never fully satisfy. Paul boldly calls them "enemies of the cross of Christ" (v. 18).

That language feels so hostile, we might miss who these "enemies" are. Paul tells us what to look for.

Their god is their stomach. (v. 19)

Don't picture people who literally worship a stomach god. (Ew.) Paul was highlighting how we all operate apart from Christ, worshipping at the twin altars of self and pleasure and seeking satisfaction in whatever feels good, tastes good, or looks good at the time. The problem here for Paul is not merely having an appetite but rather being totally *driven* by our appetites—a problem that can only be solved one way. Only Jesus can save us from the endless cycle of worshipping what we crave.

Life offers up so many "little g" gods. There are a zillion ways to seek contentment in things that can only offer temporary relief. Scripture's invitation is to turn from the gods of self and pleasure and turn our worship toward the One who "satisfies [us] with good things" (Ps. 103:5).

There's a brass-tacks difference between those who hope in Christ and those who don't. It shows up in the practicalities of life, including our approach to food. "They are focused on earthly things. Our citizenship is in heaven, and we eagerly wait for a Savior from there, the Lord Jesus Christ" (Phil. 3:19–20).

In a world obsessed with food, we are obsessed with Jesus. In a world that craves the temporary, we long for the eternal. The best bite of food on earth can't compare to what awaits us in heaven. This is the hope-filled message entrusted to us. Let's share good meals with our neighbors who do not know Him. When we do, let's say, "You think that's good? Let me introduce you to Someone even more satisfying."

SETTING THE TABLE, INVITING THE FEAST

Use the prayer prompts below to ask the Lord
to do an abundant work in your life.

Setting the Table

Jesus, sometimes I am ruled by my cravings. I see evidence of that in these situations . . .

_____

_____

_____

_____

_____

_____

_____

_____

_____

_____

_____

_____

_____

_____

_____

_____

_____

Inviting the Feast

Lord, Your Word reminds me that there are people who are driven by their appetites and are focused on earthly, temporary things because they do not know the true and eternal comfort of knowing You. Who can I offer true hope to today?

_____

_____

_____

_____

_____

_____

_____

_____

_____

_____

_____

_____

_____

_____

_____

_____

_____

_____

_____

_____

FEASTING

GLORIFIED BODIES

It is sown a natural body; it is raised a spiritual body.

—1 Corinthians 15:44 KJV

I want to do it now!"

My seven-year-old made that passionate declaration as the rest of us munched on fried shrimp. We were at the beach for a vacation. Our boy took one look at the turquoise ocean water and decided it was time—he wanted to get baptized.

We've talked to all of our children about following Jesus since long before they could talk back. He'd seen his older brothers choose to follow Christ's example in believer's baptism. He knew it was an outward expression of an inward decision to follow Jesus. There was just something about that water that spoke to his little heart. He wanted to plunge beneath its surface and come back up drenched anew in God's grace.

He bounced his way through dinner. We paid the check and headed for the beach. I stood with my toes in the sand as his daddy declared, "Judah, because of your decision to follow Jesus, I now baptize you in the name of the Father, and of the Son, and of the Holy Spirit." Ocean sprays mixed with happy tears and flowed down my face as I saw the unmatched beauty of the gospel displayed once again.

READ 1 CORINTHIANS 15:35-49.

Baptism is a picture of a kind of death. It is an expression of our faith that "[We] have been crucified with Christ, and [we] no longer live, but Christ lives in [us]" (Gal. 2:20). It's symbolic of our trust that we have been buried with Christ and risen to walk in newness of life (Rom. 6:4).

But doesn't it also point to a more physical reality? If the Lord tarries, we will die. Our physical bodies will be buried, not in blue ocean waters but in dark earth. No amount of healthy eating, carb cutting, or sugar shunning can stave off this reality forever. We need a hope that goes beyond feeling better, looking better, and getting sick less often. **We need resurrection hope.**

Compare our earthly body realities with our heavenly ones.

Our earthly bodies are:

- Sown in corruption, forever flawed by our sin nature (1 Cor. 15:42).
- Sown in dishonor, prone to run in glad rebellion away from the things of God (v. 43).
- Sown in weakness, bound to break down (v. 43).
- Sown in natural form, forced to live within the confines of broken cells (v. 44).

You can juice cleanse your way through life, eat kale at every meal, trim every ounce of fat off the bone, and these realities will remain—but a resurrection is coming!

Our heavenly bodies will be:

- Raised in incorruption, totally free of the effects of sin (v. 42).

- Raised in glory, shining like the stars in the heavens (vv. 43, 40–41).
- Raised in power, Christ's power over death (v. 44).
- Raised in a spiritual form that will never die (v. 44; Rev. 21:4).

We can live out this hope-filled truth in every area of our lives, embracing our weak bodies knowing that glorified bodies are coming. We can declare that no matter what we do, our fallen flesh is temporary, but a day is coming when we will be raised anew.

The world peddles a message that our bodies must be preserved at all costs. When Judah plunged into the ocean, he was proclaiming a more excellent way. May we join him in declaring that we're all cracked pots, and our hope is not in these pots of clay.

SETTING THE TABLE, INVITING THE FEAST

*Use the prayer prompts below to ask the Lord
to do an abundant work in your life.*

Setting the Table

*Jesus, I am prone to put too much stock in preserving my
temporary, fallen body. When I do, I always . . .*

_____

_____

_____

_____

_____

_____

Inviting the Feast

*Lord, teach me what it means to live my life in light of the
resurrection, where my body will be raised anew.*

_____

_____

_____

_____

_____

_____

_____

THE NAZARITE VOW

He is to abstain from wine and beer. He must not drink vinegar made from wine or from beer. He must not drink any grape juice or eat fresh grapes or raisins. He is not to eat anything produced by the grapevine, from seeds to skin, during the period of his consecration.

—Numbers 6:3–4

What do Samson, Samuel, John the Baptist, and Paul hold in common? Well, for one thing, they didn't eat raisins.

Numbers 6 outlines the parameters of a commitment the Israelites could voluntarily make called the Nazarite vow. It was a pledge to follow a specific set of restrictions as an expression of a desire to live set apart for the Lord.

READ NUMBERS 6:1–21.

Samson took the vow (Judg. 16:17), which is why the shaving of his head at the hand of Delilah was such a big (hairy) deal. The prophets Samuel and John the Baptist also took the Nazarite vow (1 Sam. 1:11;

Luke 1:15). The New Testament records that the apostle Paul took the vow even after his conversion (Acts 18:18).

I don't know about you, but I tend to get wrapped up in the long hair part of these verses. Let's look again and take note. Instructions for the Nazarite vow didn't begin with the more peculiar directions about hairdos and dealing with the dead. *They started with food.*

To be crystal clear, this passage is not forbidding wine, beer, vinegar, grape juice, fresh grapes, or raisins for all of God's people all the time. Jesus Himself ate and drank many of the items on that list. Once again we see that when it comes to food, when it comes to everything, God is less concerned with our lists of "dos and don'ts" and most concerned with our devotion.

Vow or no vow, to follow Jesus is to live set apart.

This is why Scripture pleads,

> Therefore, brothers and sisters, in view of the mercies of God, I urge you to present your bodies as a living sacrifice, holy and pleasing to God; this is your true worship. Do not be conformed to this age, but be transformed by the renewing of your mind, so that you may discern what is the good, pleasing, and perfect will of God. (Rom. 12:1–2)

The Nazarite vow was given by God in the same spirit as Scripture's call to embrace fasting. It's voluntary. God's never gonna make us. The vow was an opportunity to take the initiative to live marked for God's glory. *Fasting is an opportunity to take the initiative to live marked for God's glory.*

Pause and consider: What do the Christ followers you admire most have in common? They may or may not eat raisins, but I am sure of this—they don't try to be like everyone else; their goal is not to blend in with a world that doesn't recognize Jesus. They live consecrated lives, dedicated to God's glory. That's the heart of the Nazarite vow. That's the heart of fasting.

> But as the one who called you is holy, you also are to be holy in all your conduct. (1 Pet. 1:15)

SETTING THE TABLE, INVITING THE FEAST

*Use the prayer prompts below to ask the Lord
to do an abundant work in your life.*

Setting the Table

*Jesus, I want to live set apart for You. Specifically, I know I need to
make changes in the area of . . .*

_____

_____

_____

_____

_____

Inviting the Feast

*Lord, it's so much easier to live like everyone else. Forgive me for
wanting to fit in more than I've wanted to live like You call me to.
Show me just how joyful and satisfying it is to live only for Your glory
and purposes.*

_____

_____

_____

_____

_____

_____

_____

FEAS T I N G

FEED MY SHEEP

"Feed my sheep."
—John 21:17

Sometimes life rafts come in the shape of a nine-by-twelve pan.
Several years ago, the patriarch of our family died unexpectedly in his sleep. Before we even had time to wrap our heads around our sorrow, food started showing up at our door. Friends brought boxes of fried chicken and fixins. Family members brought cakes and cinnamon rolls. Church members brought stacks of paper plates and shrink-wrapped juice boxes. It was a comfort too profound for me to put into words.

We needed something stronger than a slice of pie to assuage our grief, but the food gifts meant that someone was thinking about us, someone was praying for us, and that meant we were going to be okay.

READ JOHN 21:15–19.

After Jesus cooked His disciples breakfast (v. 12), He pulled Peter aside to teach him how to pick up the mantle of leading the church.

There was no five-point sermon, no master class on discipleship. Jesus' instructions were jarringly simple, "Feed my sheep."

Of course, Jesus was telling Peter to meet people's spiritual hunger, but as we've already seen so often in Scripture, body and soul are not divorced. Many times Jesus met physical needs before He even addressed spiritual ones. We can serve one another by feeding stomachs and souls.

I once read a hyperbole about two groups of people, each gathered at round tables piled high with every delectable food. Their spoons were so long they could not reach their mouths. One group was miserable because they could not find a way to eat. The other group was too busy feasting to notice. They learned to feed one another.

Church, we are the second group. Yes, we feed one another truth. We feed one another purpose. We feed one another encouragement. But can't we also commit to the other kind of feeding? Can we take freezer meals to new mommas and soup to sick friends? Can we drop off thinking-of-you cookies and I'm-praying-for-you cinnamon rolls? There is comfort in food. There is ministry in food.

Do you love Jesus? Of course you do!

Feed His lambs. The feast of Christian fellowship begins when we learn to feed one another.

SETTING THE TABLE, INVITING THE FEAST

*Use the prayer prompts below to ask the Lord
to do an abundant work in your life.*

Setting the Table

*Jesus, I have been blessed by food gifts in the past. Bring someone
to mind whom I can thank for that blessing today.*

_____

_____

_____

_____

_____

_____

_____

_____

_____

_____

_____

_____

_____

_____

_____

_____

_____

Inviting the Feast

Lord, I want to serve You by serving others. Whom can I feed today?

THE MARRIAGE SUPPER OF THE LAMB

"Write: Blessed are those invited to the marriage feast of the Lamb!"

—Revelation 19:9

Tell me I'm not the only one who wears stretchy pants on Thanksgiving Day in anticipation of the feast. Even that silly habit can preach to our hearts about a deeper truth.

READ REVELATION 19:1–10.

God is moving time toward the moment described in these verses, the marriage supper of the Lamb. I'm not sure if we will literally feed our glorified bodies or not. I do know that when God inspired John to write about life behind the veil of heaven, a feast is the picture He chose.

Let's imagine what it will be like when our sin has been removed from our lives (v. 2). Try to picture the scene of creatures great and small unified in praise to the one true King (v. 4). Imagine what it will sound like when the voices of the saints are so many and so loud, we sound like Niagara Falls as we declare, "Hallelujah, because our Lord God, the Almighty, reigns!" (v. 6).

What will heaven's food taste like? What could adorn the tables of the King of kings?

> What no eye has seen, no ear has heard,
> and no human heart conceived—
> God has prepared these things for those who love him.
> (1 Cor. 2:9)

We've never seen anything like it.

We've never heard anything like it.

We've never imagined anything like what our heavenly Groom has in store for us, His bride.

Remember when Jesus said His disciples would start fasting?

> Jesus said to them, "Can the wedding guests be sad while the groom is with them? The time will come when the groom will be taken away from them, and then they will fast." (Matt. 9:15)

Only when we are finally and forever reunited with our Groom will fasting have served its purpose. Only then will the true feasting begin.

A pastor once said it this way, "In fasting, we confess we are not home yet, and remember that we are not homeless. In fasting, we cry out to our Groom, and remember that we have his covenant promises. In fasting, we confess our lack, and remember that the one with every resource has pledged his help in his perfect timing."[7]

Few practices can remind us how earthbound we are quicker than fasting. Missing a single meal causes our stomachs to grumble and our minds to obsess over food. If we fast longer, our blood sugar drops, our brains get foggy, and every food item in our pantry seems to start calling our name. These physical pangs are also reminders of a greater reality. In fasting we force our bodies to testify and our hearts to fixate on the truth that it will not always be this way.

A feast is coming, friend. The Bread of Life will be ours to behold. The Living Water will quench our thirst (Rev. 21:6; 22:17). Like wearing stretchy pants on Thanksgiving, Scripture's call is to hold on to life loosely in anticipation of the wedding feast to come.

SETTING THE TABLE, INVITING THE FEAST

*Use the prayer prompts below to ask the Lord
to do an abundant work in your life.*

Setting the Table

Jesus, I cannot wait to be with You in the new heaven and new earth. Some of the things I am looking forward to most are . . .

_____

_____

_____

_____

_____

_____

_____

_____

_____

_____

_____

Inviting the Feast

Lord, I want my life to cry out to You, my Groom, and declare Your covenant promises as I wait to be with You forever. Show me how I can do that more and more.

Write down whatever comes to mind.

_____

_____

_____

_____

_____

_____

_____

_____

_____

_____

_____

_____

_____

_____

_____

_____

_____

_____

_____

FASTING AND FEASTING

LIKE A DRINK OFFERING

For I am already being poured out as a drink offering,
and the time for my departure is close.

—2 Timothy 4:6

As I write this final devotional, we are two-thirds through the Lenten season. Though observing Lent is a church tradition, not a biblical mandate, my faith muscles have been strengthened through the years by the practice of setting aside the forty days leading up to Resurrection Sunday to fast from food and feast on the Lord.

Pay attention to those last four words, "feast on the Lord." Let them press deep into every crevice of your heart. If we just cut something out of our lives, we miss the point. Deprivation for deprivation's sake is not what Jesus modeled or called us to. The heart of true fasting is to make room for feasting on God's presence, on His Word, on His truth.

Why didn't God give us a manual like so many other voices speaking about food are so willing to do? Why didn't He tell us to fast these days and feast those days? Why give us theory and not mandate the practice? Because to embrace the rhythms of fasting and feasting is to commit to walk by the Spirit.

Once again, Paul is using food language to help us understand the way of Jesus. Paul wrote these words from prison during his final days on earth. What word picture did he use to describe his life? What image did he want to leave with those who were watching his faith lived out? The image of a drink being slowly spilled out.

> For I am already being poured out as a drink offering. (v. 6)

Jesus fills us with His love. We pour His love back out into the hearts of others. Jesus fills us with His truth. We drench a deceived world with it. Jesus satisfies us with His Word. We tip the cup by living out what He shows us. Paul's words are true of each of us seeking to showcase God's glory in the way we live our lives. For we are already being poured out as a drink offering.

God may want to use His Word to defibrillate some things about your relationship with food. Perhaps He's calling you to fast in order to express your commitment to live for Him. (He's certainly given us strong reasons to consider fasting in His Word.) Maybe He's calling you to feast, to let go of your presumptions that food is bad and to enjoy the good gifts He's placed on your table. Very likely it's a combination.

Fasting and feasting; feasting and fasting. Filled up and poured out. These are the food patterns we find in the pages of our Bible. They can spill right over onto our tables and our grocery lists, into the way we live our lives as we seek to follow Jesus. The goal of both rhythms is the same—more of Jesus, less of us, more of the satisfying taste of His presence, less of the things that can never fill us up.

Whether fasting or feasting, to walk in the Spirit is to embrace a life that declares:

Who do I have in heaven but you?
And I desire nothing on earth but you.
My flesh and my heart may fail,
but God is the strength of my heart,
my portion forever. (Ps. 73:25–26)

Let's dig in.

SETTING THE TABLE, INVITING THE FEAST

*Use the prayer prompts below to ask the Lord
to do an abundant work in your life.*

Setting the Table

*Jesus, I want more of You. More of Your truth. More of Your
presence in my life. I want to be poured out.*

_____

_____

_____

_____

Inviting the Feast

*Lord, are there places in my heart that You want to defibrillate? Are
there things about my relationship with food that You need to shock
back into rhythm? Show me what they are.*

Write down anything that comes to mind.

_____

_____

_____

_____

_____

_____

_____

NOTES

1. John Piper, *God's Passion for His Glory: Living the Vision of Jonathan Edwards* (Wheaton, IL: Crossway, 1998), 75.

2. Piper, *God's Passion for His Glory*, 47.

3. Grace Enstrom, "An Intrinsic Love for the Craft," February 26, 2021, https://gracebyenstrom.com/story.

4. "10 Animals That Can Live without Food and Water for Months," *The Times of India*, January 24, 2018, https://recipes.timesofindia.com/us/articles/features/10-animals-that-can-live-without-food-and-water-for-months/photostory/62636198.cms.

5. A. W. Tozer, *The Knowledge of the Holy* (New York: HarperCollins, 1961).

6. "Interesting Facts about Coriander," Just Fun Facts, February 26, 2021, http://justfunfacts.com/interesting-facts-about-coriander.

7. David Mathis, "Why Do Christians Fast?," Desiring God, September 26, 2018, https://www.desiringgod.org/articles/why-do-christians-fast.

Also available from
ERIN DAVIS

BIBLE STUDIES FOR TEEN GIRLS

Beautiful Encounters   *True Princess*   *Beautiful Story*

BOOKS FOR WOMEN

Connected

AVAILABLE WHEREVER BOOKS ARE SOLD

the
DEEP
WELL
with Erin Davis

FALL IN LOVE
WITH YOUR WHOLE BIBLE

God's Word is a deep well. You can drop down your bucket
and pull up truth every time. Keep opening your Bible alongside
Erin with her podcast, **The Deep Well with Erin Davis**.

Find it on your favorite podcast app.